I0090180

Edward Snowden

Edward Snowden

STATE ENEMY OR PRIVACY DEFENDER?

GEW Intelligence Unit

HICHEM KAROUI (ED.)

Global East-West (London)

Copyright © 2024 by GEW Intelligence Unit

Hichem Karoui (Editor)

Global East-West (London)

All rights reserved. No part of this book may be reproduced in any manner whatsoever without written permission except in the case of brief quotations embodied in critical articles and reviews.

First Printing, 2024

Contents

Contents

The Blueprint of Surveillance: A Prelude

Modern Surveillance

The landscape of modern surveillance encompasses a wide array of techniques and technologies employed to monitor individuals, groups, and activities. At its core, modern surveillance involves the systematic observation, recording, and analysis of behaviors, communications, locations, or other attributes of targeted subjects. In today's interconnected world, surveillance extends beyond physical spaces to include digital realms, giving rise to the concept of digital surveillance or cyber-surveillance. This form of surveillance entails the collection and scrutiny of electronic data, including online interactions, browsing activities, and digital footprints. The proliferation of digital devices, from smartphones to IoT (Internet of Things) gadgets, has further broadened the scope of surveillance, ushering in an era where everyday objects can serve as conduits for monitoring and data collection. Key terminologies in modern surveillance include 'metadata', which comprises the contextual information about a communication or data; 'mass surveillance', referring to the indiscriminate interception and analysis of information on a large scale; and 'surveillance capitalism', a concept that underscores the commodification of personal data by technology firms for commercial purposes. As surveillance methodologies have advanced, the ethical implications of these practices have become increasingly complex. The convergence of emerging technologies such as artificial intelligence and facial recognition with surveillance capabilities raises critical concerns regarding privacy, civil liberties, and the potential for societal control. Understanding the mechanisms and terminologies underpinning modern surveillance is essential for grasping the intricate dynamics at play in contemporary society, as well as the implications that Edward Snowden's disclosures would come to expose.

Historical Context of Surveillance Techniques

Surveillance has been an integral part of human societies for centuries, with historical records revealing various techniques used to gather information and monitor individuals or groups. The earliest forms of surveillance can be traced back to ancient civilizations, where rulers employed messengers, spies, and informants to keep a close watch on their subjects and enemies. These methods were often primitive but effective in maintaining control and ensuring the security of the ruling class. As societies evolved, so did surveillance techniques. The Roman Empire, for example, utilized an extensive network of informants, known as 'delators,' who reported disloyalty and dissent to the authorities. This model of using civilians to spy on one another became a recurring feature in the history of surveillance. The Middle Ages saw the establishment of formal intelligence agencies, such as the Venetian secret service, which engaged in covert operations to protect the interests of the Republic. During the Renaissance, the use of coded messages and invisible ink became prevalent, marking a shift towards more sophisticated surveillance methods. The advent of industrialization and urbanization in the 19th century further amplified the need for surveillance, as governments sought to exert greater control over their increasingly populous and diverse populations. The utilization of photography and telegraphy enabled authorities to gather and disseminate information more rapidly than ever before. The 20th century witnessed unprecedented advancements in surveillance technology, particularly during times of global conflict. Both World War I and World War II saw the widespread use of wiretapping, aerial reconnaissance, and propaganda to gather intelligence and sway public opinion. The aftermath of these conflicts led to the Cold War era, characterized by heightened surveillance efforts on a global scale. The proliferation of surveillance cameras, hidden microphones, and espionage activities underscored the intense competition between rival powers. As the digital age dawned, surveillance entered a new frontier, with the exponential growth of electronic communication and data storage. The rise of the internet and the development of sophisticated algorithms revolutionized the surveillance landscape, enabling the mass collection and analysis of personal information. In this historical context, surveillance has continuously adapted and expanded, reflecting the evolving capabilities of those seeking to observe, influence, and control others.

Technological Evolution in Data Gathering

The proliferation of digital technology has precipitated a revolution in data gathering methods, fundamentally reshaping the landscape of surveillance. With the advent of the internet and the widespread adoption of digital devices, the volume and diversity of data being collected have surged exponentially. The transition from analog to digital systems has not only increased the ease and precision of data collection but has also expanded the avenues through which personal information can be acquired. This shift has allowed for the comprehensive monitoring of individuals' digital footprints, encompassing online activities, communication patterns, browsing histories, and even location data. Moreover, the integration of sophisticated data mining and analysis tools has empowered entities, both public and private, to extract actionable insights from the colossal datasets amassed through various digital channels. Algorithms capable of processing vast amounts of raw data have enabled the identification of behavioral patterns, correlations, and trends, granting surveillance initiatives the capacity to predict and preempt certain behaviors or events with unprecedented accuracy. Simultaneously, advancements in sensor technologies, including closed-circuit television (CCTV), facial recognition systems, and biometric scanners, have augmented the physical scope of surveillance. These tools facilitate the continuous monitoring and identification of individuals in public spaces, effectively eroding traditional notions of anonymity and privacy. Concurrently, the omnipresence of interconnected smart devices and the internet of things (IoT) has engendered a new paradigm of ubiquitous surveillance, wherein everyday objects are embedded with sensors that continuously collect and transmit data regarding users' behaviors and environments. From smart home devices to wearable technology, these interconnected systems generate copious amounts of data that, when aggregated and analyzed, offer detailed insights into individuals' lives. This technological evolution has not only propelled the capabilities of surveillance mechanisms but has also ushered in ethical and legal dilemmas surrounding the extent of permissible data gathering, potential misuse of collected information, and the implications for individual privacy and autonomy. As such, understanding the intricacies and implications of this transformative era in data gathering is essential for comprehending the context within which Edward Snowden's disclosures took place.

Governmental Role in Surveillance Expansion

The expansion of surveillance capabilities has been significantly influenced by the active involvement of governments around the world. As technological advancements have rapidly transformed the landscape of information gathering, governments have played a central role in driving and funding the development of surveillance technologies. Through various agencies and initiatives, governments have actively promoted the enhancement of surveillance capabilities for purposes such as national security, law enforcement, and intelligence gathering. Governmental organizations have collaborated with private entities to foster the growth of surveillance infrastructure. This collaboration has led to the allocation of substantial resources towards research and development in the field of surveillance technology. Furthermore, governments have often provided legal and financial support to private companies engaged in the creation of sophisticated surveillance tools, thereby contributing to the proliferation of surveillance mechanisms in both domestic and international contexts. The legislative and regulatory actions of governments have also played a pivotal role in shaping the parameters within which surveillance activities operate. Statutory frameworks, such as anti-terrorism laws and intelligence legislation, have been employed to justify and authorize the expansion of surveillance powers granted to government agencies. These legal provisions have, in turn, facilitated the deployment of surveillance technologies on a wide scale, often without robust mechanisms for oversight and accountability. Moreover, governmental intelligence and security agencies have been instrumental in advancing surveillance strategies that extend beyond traditional boundaries. By leveraging their authority and expertise, these agencies have cultivated a global network of surveillance operations, presenting challenges to privacy rights and civil liberties on an international scale. The collaborative efforts between government bodies have contributed to the seamless integration of surveillance systems across borders, raising critical questions about the ethical and legal implications of such transnational practices. The growing influence of government-sponsored surveillance programs has given rise to debates concerning the balance between security imperatives and individual privacy rights. While proponents argue that effective surveillance measures are essential for safeguarding national interests and protecting citizens from potential threats, critics contend that unchecked governmental surveillance encroaches upon fundamental freedoms and poses risks of abuse and overreach. In light of the governmental involvement in surveillance expansion, it becomes paramount to critically examine the implications of the evolving surveillance landscape and explore the complex interplay between state interests, technological capabilities, and ethical considerations.

Legal Frameworks Governing Privacy and Surveillance

The legal framework governing privacy and surveillance is a complex web of regulations, laws, and international agreements that seek to balance the need for security with individual rights to privacy. In modern democracies, this balance is often hotly debated in legal circles, as well as in the public arena, due to the rapid evolution of technology and its impact on surveillance capabilities. At the core of the legal framework are foundational documents such as constitutions, charters of rights and freedoms, and international human rights conventions, which enshrine the right to privacy as a fundamental human right. However, these rights are tested by the broad powers granted to intelligence agencies, law enforcement bodies, and governments to collect and analyze data in the name of national security. One key aspect of the legal framework is the concept of probable cause, which serves to limit unwarranted intrusion into individuals' private lives. This principle requires that authorities have credible evidence indicating that a person may be involved in criminal activity before conducting surveillance. Additionally, oversight mechanisms, such as specialized courts or review boards, play an essential role in ensuring that surveillance activities comply with legal standards. These oversight bodies are tasked with assessing the necessity and proportionality of surveillance measures, thereby safeguarding individuals from arbitrary or excessive intrusion. Furthermore, privacy laws and regulations dictate the boundaries within which personal data can be collected, processed, and shared. These laws often include provisions for informed consent, data minimization, purpose limitation, and data security, aiming to protect individuals from unauthorized access or misuse of their information. Moreover, international human rights instruments, such as the European Convention on Human Rights and the International Covenant on Civil and Political Rights, require states to uphold the right to privacy and establish effective remedies for privacy violations. Transnational data sharing and cross-border surveillance present additional challenges, prompting the development of mutual legal assistance treaties and international agreements to govern cooperation among countries. However, the rapid advancement of surveillance technologies and their global reach have sparked debates over the adequacy of existing legal frameworks to address emerging threats to privacy. Contemporary issues, including mass collection of telecommunications metadata, facial recognition, and encrypted communication, pose new challenges to traditional legal safeguards. As such, lawmakers and courts face the arduous task of adapting legal standards to reflect technological advancements while upholding fundamental principles of privacy. Addressing these challenges requires ongoing dialogue between legal experts, policymakers, and technologists to ensure that the legal framework remains relevant and effective in the digital age.

Global Surveillance Dynamics

The spectrum of global surveillance dynamics encompasses a complex web of interconnected systems, ranging from governmental intelligence agencies to private entities in various sectors. The digital age has witnessed an unprecedented surge in the volume and diversity of data being collected, processed, and utilized for surveillance purposes across international borders. This section aims to delve into the multifaceted elements that contribute to the global surveillance landscape. At the heart of global surveillance dynamics is the intricate interplay between national security interests and individual privacy rights. Governments continually seek to enhance their intelligence capabilities to combat emerging threats, whether they be related to terrorism, cyber espionage, or geopolitical tensions. As a result, surveillance practices have evolved and expanded, utilizing advanced technologies to monitor communication networks, financial transactions, and movement patterns on a global scale. Moreover, the proliferation of surveillance extends beyond the public sector, with private enterprises also wielding significant influence in this domain. Technology companies, telecommunications providers, and data brokers are key players in the surveillance industry, as their products and services are instrumental in the collection and analysis of vast amounts of personal and behavioral data. The convergence of these commercial interests with state surveillance objectives further complicates the regulatory and ethical considerations surrounding global surveillance dynamics. In addition to technological advancements, the legal and diplomatic dimensions of surveillance play a pivotal role in shaping its global dynamics. International agreements, treaties, and bilateral cooperation frameworks define the parameters within which surveillance activities are conducted and exchanged among nations. However, challenges arise when differing legal standards and cultural norms collide, leading to friction and disputes that impact cross-border surveillance practices. Furthermore, the revelations of pervasive mass surveillance programs, such as those disclosed by Edward Snowden, have sparked intense debates about the balance between security imperatives and civil liberties on a global scale. These disclosures have brought to light the extent to which surveillance technologies can be exploited for purposes beyond their intended scope, raising profound concerns about overreach and abuse of power. Ultimately, understanding the intricacies of global surveillance dynamics requires a comprehensive examination of its technological, political, legal, and ethical facets. It is imperative to navigate through this complexity with a discerning lens, analyzing the implications and ramifications of surveillance practices in an increasingly connected world.

Key Players in the Surveillance Industry

The landscape of global surveillance is shaped by a myriad of organizations and entities that play pivotal roles in the development, implementation, and proliferation of surveillance technologies. These key players operate across various sectors, including governmental, corporate, and technological domains, influencing the way surveillance is conducted and its impact on individuals and societies. Within the governmental sphere, intelligence agencies and law enforcement bodies are prominent stakeholders in the surveillance industry. These organizations often have access to significant resources, enabling them to engage in extensive data collection and analysis activities. Their utilization of advanced surveillance tools and techniques is instrumental in maintaining national security and combating criminal activities, but it also raises critical concerns regarding privacy infringement and civil liberties. From a corporate perspective, technology companies occupy a central position in the surveillance ecosystem. Companies specializing in software development, telecommunications, and information technology contribute to the innovation and deployment of surveillance infrastructures. As providers of digital platforms and communication services, these entities possess substantial influence over the data streams that form the basis of modern surveillance practices. Moreover, their involvement in initiatives such as data mining, predictive analytics, and algorithmic monitoring has far-reaching implications for consumer privacy and data protection. The intertwining of government and corporate interests further underscores the complexities inherent in contemporary surveillance landscapes. In addition to state and corporate actors, non-governmental organizations and advocacy groups play a crucial role in shaping the discourse around surveillance. Civil society entities dedicated to privacy rights, digital freedom, and transparency efforts actively monitor and scrutinize the behavior of powerful surveillance entities. Moreover, they often serve as catalysts for policy debates and legal reforms aimed at safeguarding individual liberties in the face of expanding surveillance capabilities. By advocating for oversight mechanisms, accountability frameworks, and transparency measures, these entities seek to mitigate the potential abuses associated with unchecked surveillance practices. Beyond the known entities, emerging players in the surveillance industry, such as cybersecurity firms and data brokers, are increasingly influential in defining the contours of contemporary surveillance landscapes. Their contributions to threat intelligence, cyber defense, and data monetization fundamentally shape the dynamics of surveillance operations in the digital age. In light of their growing significance, understanding the motives, practices, and interconnections of these key players is imperative in comprehending the broader implications of surveillance on privacy, security, and human rights.

Ethics and Challenges in Digital Surveillance

In the rapidly evolving landscape of digital surveillance, ethical considerations and challenges loom large, casting profound implications on privacy, civil liberties, and the balance of power between individuals and institutions. As technology continues to advance at an unprecedented pace, the ethical dimensions of surveillance practices have become increasingly complex and contentious. Fundamental questions about the permissible extent of data collection, the justifiability of mass surveillance, and the protection of individual rights in an era of pervasive monitoring have ignited fervent debates across global jurisdictions. The ubiquity of digital surveillance tools has ushered in an era where privacy is inherently vulnerable, giving rise to ethical dilemmas that demand a delicate balance between security imperatives and the preservation of personal freedoms. The expansive reach of surveillance technologies, encompassing everything from network interceptions and data mining to facial recognition and biometric tracking, presents multifaceted ethical challenges pertaining to consent, transparency, and accountability. Within this context, the ethical implications of utilizing surveillance for purposes such as crime prevention, national security, and public safety intersect with profound concerns regarding potential abuses of power, erosion of privacy, and the chilling effects on free expression and dissent. Moreover, the interconnectedness of digital ecosystems has intensified global interconnectedness and exposed individuals to unprecedented levels of scrutiny. This has precipitated ethical quandaries concerning the international governance of surveillance activities, especially in light of differing cultural norms, legal frameworks, and regulatory approaches across nations. The formidable ethical considerations also extend to the commercial realm, given the proliferation of private entities engaged in extensive data collection and analysis. These practices raise pressing questions about corporate responsibility, the commodification of personal information, and the ethical boundaries governing the monetization of individual digital footprints. Evidently, navigating the ethical intricacies of digital surveillance demands a nuanced understanding of not only the technological capabilities but also the moral imperative to safeguard privacy, dignity, and autonomy. Striking a harmonious equilibrium between the imperatives of security and the ethical red lines demarcating fundamental human rights remains an intricate challenge faced by policymakers, industry stakeholders, and society at large.

Major Revelations Prior to Snowden

In the years leading up to Edward Snowden's momentous disclosures, a series of significant revelations had already shed light on the extent of digital surveillance and its ramifications. One notable precursor to Snowden's revelations was the disclosure of the NSA's warrantless wiretapping program in 2005 by The New York Times. This revelation provided a glimpse into the government's expansive surveillance practices, setting the stage for later disclosures. Similarly, the emergence of WikiLeaks and its publication of sensitive government documents, including the 'Collateral Murder' video, highlighted the potential impact of whistleblowing on public awareness and discourse. Moreover, the release of documents by Chelsea Manning, then known as Bradley Manning, through WikiLeaks offered insights into the military's actions and diplomatic relations, casting a spotlight on government transparency and accountability. These earlier revelations served as critical precursors, laying the groundwork for the seismic disclosures that would follow in the wake of Edward Snowden's actions.

Setting the Stage for Edward Snowden's Disclosures

The period preceding Edward Snowden's disclosures was characterized by various significant events and milestones that sowed the seeds for his revelations. These events were instrumental in shaping the landscape of surveillance, privacy, and government oversight during that time. The stage for Snowden's disclosures was set against a backdrop of growing concerns regarding the scope and intrusion of state-sponsored surveillance programs across the globe. During this era, there were a number of high-profile incidents that brought attention to the pervasive nature of surveillance activities. Notably, the public learned about the warrantless wiretapping program initiated by the National Security Agency (NSA) following the 9/11 attacks, exposing the extent to which government agencies were conducting electronic surveillance on both domestic and international communications without clear legal authority. Additionally, revelations about the proliferation of mass data collection programs and the utilization of advanced technologies for intelligence gathering further underscored the expanding capabilities of surveillance apparatuses. This climate of heightened awareness and scrutiny set the groundwork for the impact that Edward Snowden's disclosures would have on public discourse and global policies concerning privacy and civil liberties. Moreover, it highlighted the increasing tension between national security imperatives and individual rights to privacy. In parallel, debates surrounding the use of surveillance technologies encompassed ethical considerations, accountability mechanisms, and the evolving role of technology companies in facilitating government access to personal data. The interplay between these factors informed the environment in which Edward Snowden made his fateful decision to unveil classified information and shed light on the far-reaching extent of government surveillance programs. As such, his actions would disrupt the existing paradigm and catalyze widespread reevaluation of surveillance practices and their implications for democratic societies.

2

Who is Edward Snowden? Early Life and Career

Overview

Edward Snowden, a figure who would come to exemplify the complexities of modern-day surveillance and privacy, was born on June 21, 1983, in Elizabeth City, North Carolina. His family background, rooted in the middle-class ethos of patriotism and public service, would lay the foundation for his eventual journey into the world of intelligence and whistleblowing. Snowden's childhood, shaped by an environment that valued integrity and questioned authority, instilled in him a deep sense of moral responsibility. As he navigated the landscapes of adolescence and young adulthood, his understanding of global events and the pervasive impact of government actions ingrained within him an unwavering commitment to truth and justice. Through his formative years, Snowden witnessed the repercussions of unchecked power and the potential for widespread harm caused by clandestine activities. The close-knit fabric of his family provided a safe space for open discourse and intellectual exploration, nurturing within him a curiosity about the intersection of technology, privacy, and civil liberties. This upbringing set the stage for his later endeavors. Snowden's early experiences with digital technology and computing, combined with an insatiable thirst for knowledge, led him down a path characterized by technical expertise and analytical acumen. The foundational values instilled during his upbringing merged with a burgeoning aptitude for innovative problem-solving, forging a unique perspective that would fuel his future actions. These aspects of his background shed light on the intricate tapestry of influences that ultimately shaped and propelled Edward Snowden toward the pivotal role he would come to play in the landscape of global surveillance and individual privacy. Motivated by a desire to bring transparency and accountability to the forefront of public discourse, Snowden embarked on a path driven by a profound belief in the principles of democratic governance and the fundamental rights of individuals. It is through this lens of conviction and foresight that his journey unfolds, unveiling the intricate layers of ethical considerations, personal sacrifice, and the irrepressible spirit of dedication to the greater good.

Birth and Family Background

Edward Joseph Snowden was born on June 21, 1983, in Elizabeth City, North Carolina, to parents Lonnie Snowden and Elizabeth B. Snowden. He was raised in a family deeply rooted in military and public service, with both of his grandfathers having served in the United States Coast Guard. This familial influence played a significant role in shaping Snowden's values and principles. The environment at home emphasized discipline, duty, and patriotism, instilling in Snowden a strong sense of civic responsibility from a young age. His family's ethos of service to the nation became an integral part of his character and would later inform his decision-making during the pivotal events that unfolded in his life. Edward Snowden's formative years were marked by the steady influence of his close-knit family. As he navigated his early experiences and interacted with the world around him, the values and traditions upheld within the Snowden household laid the ground-work for the ideals that would ultimately drive his actions as an adult. Understanding the foundation that his upbringing provided is essential to comprehending the depth and conviction behind Edward Snowden's later choices. His family background serves as a crucial backdrop against which his future trajectory would unfold, shedding light on the roots of the ethical and moral compass that guided his path through life.

Education and Formative Years

Edward Snowden's formative years were characterized by a voracious appetite for learning and an unwavering dedication to understanding complex systems. Although not formally educated until the age of six, Snowden exhibited exceptional intellectual curiosity from a young age. As a child, he often immersed himself in books about technology, displaying a particular fascination with computers and their inner workings. His early years were marked by a deep interest in understanding the rapidly evolving digital landscape, leading him to independently explore various programming languages and computer hardware configurations. Snowden's interactions with technology during his youth laid the foundation for his future endeavors in the intelligence field.

Technological Proficiency and Early Interests

Edward Snowden's early years were marked by an exceptional aptitude for technology, which would later become a defining aspect of his identity and career. As a young child, he displayed an insatiable curiosity for all things related to computers and the rapidly emerging digital world. His fascination with technology led him to immerse himself in learning about programming, software development, and computer systems, driven by an innate desire to understand and manipulate these tools. In his formative years, while many of his peers were engrossed in traditional childhood activities, Snowden was already delving into the inner workings of computers and networks, demonstrating a precocious intellect and an intuitive grasp of complex technological concepts. This unparalleled enthusiasm for technology set him apart from his peers and laid the foundation for his future endeavors. Snowden's early interests not only encompassed technical mastery but also extended to a keen awareness of the potential societal implications of rapidly advancing digital systems. Throughout his adolescence, he began to contemplate the ethical and moral dimensions of the burgeoning digital landscape as he grappled with issues of privacy, security, and the ever-expanding reach of technology into everyday life. This nascent awareness sowed the seeds for his later convictions and the profound impact he would have on global conversations surrounding surveillance and privacy. Snowden's unwavering dedication to understanding and harnessing technology played a pivotal role in shaping his worldview and ultimately set the stage for the momentous decisions that lay ahead.

Military Service Attempt and Injuries

Edward Snowden's aspiration to serve in the United States military was a deeply entrenched part of his personal ethos. However, this ambition faced an abrupt halt due to physical injuries he sustained during an intensive training session. The setback occurred when Snowden, with unwavering determination, was pursuing his dream of joining the Special Forces. The rigorous demands of the military training took a toll on his body, resulting in significant injuries that permanently dashed his immediate hopes of serving in the armed forces.

This unexpected turn of events posed a profound challenge to Snowden, forcing him to reassess and adapt his aspirations for the future. Despite the disappointment and physical limitations imposed by the injuries, Snowden displayed resilience and channeled his focus towards leveraging his intellectual prowess in other arenas. It was during this pivotal period of convalescence that Snowden gravitated towards the world of technology and information systems, recognizing the potential for making a profound impact through alternative means.

The difficulties he encountered during his fervent pursuit of military service instilled in Snowden a renewed sense of purpose and zeal, propelling him into a realm where intellect and proficiency held as much significance as physical endurance. This chapter of setbacks and recovery would indelibly shape Edwards Snowden's path, ultimately leading him to emerge as a central figure in the global discourse surrounding surveillance, privacy, and government accountability.

Entrance into the Intelligence Community

After recovering from the injuries sustained during his training, Edward Snowden was drawn to the realm of intelligence and cybersecurity. His natural aptitude for technology and his unwavering commitment to public service drove him to seek opportunities within the intelligence community. Snowden exhibited a remarkable blend of technical prowess and ethical conviction that made him an attractive candidate for such roles. In pursuit of his aspirations, he pursued various certifications and training programs related to cybersecurity and information technology, actively honing his skills in these domains. As he delved deeper into the world of cybersecurity, Snowden's reputation as a proficient and principled individual began to precede him, laying the foundation for his eventual ingress into the intelligence landscape. Snowden's fervent dedication and keen insight into the evolving landscape of digital security positioned him as a promising prospect within the intelligence community. His unwavering determination and discerning intellect set the stage for the pivotal role he would come to play within the National Security Agency (NSA) and the Central Intelligence Agency (CIA). Through meticulous efforts and scholarly pursuits, Snowden carved a path for himself, driven by an unyielding sense of duty and a profound commitment to safeguarding the ideals of privacy and freedom. This period marked the gradual but steadfast integration of Edward Snowden into the fabric of the intelligence community, a trajectory that would ultimately intersect with matters of profound consequence on the global stage.

Roles and Responsibilities at NSA and CIA

Edward Snowden's tenure within the National Security Agency (NSA) and the Central Intelligence Agency (CIA) was characterized by an array of pivotal roles and significant responsibilities. As a contractual employee for the NSA, Snowden exercised his expertise in various technical capacities, which included his contributions to critical infrastructure and security protocols. Within this role, he was entrusted with the management of extensive databases containing sensitive information, allowing him access to a breadth of intelligence operations and programs.

Simultaneously, his association with the CIA equipped him with an insider's perspective on clandestine operations, intelligence analysis, and covert missions. Having demonstrated an exceptional proficiency in computer systems and digital networks, Snowden played a crucial role in cyber operations and surveillance initiatives, contributing to the development and maintenance of cutting-edge technology instrumental in the intelligence community's functions. Furthermore, his involvement in the design and implementation of data collection mechanisms positioned him at the heart of the complex web of global monitoring activities conducted by these agencies.

As Snowden navigated his responsibilities at the intersecting domains of the NSA and the CIA, he gained invaluable insights into the inner workings of the U.S. intelligence apparatus. His in-depth immersion in these organizations allowed him to witness the extent of the surveillance reach, both domestically and internationally, raising ethical quandaries that would ultimately shape his trajectory as a whistleblower. Through this meticulous exposition of his formidable roles and towering responsibilities, it becomes evident that Snowden's experiences were formative in catalyzing his profound disillusionment with the systemic overreach of surveillance practices, igniting a chain of events that would reverberate throughout history.

Growing Disillusionment with Surveillance Practices

Edward Snowden's immersion in the intelligence community provided him with a firsthand and intricate understanding of surveillance practices. As he delved deeper into his roles at the National Security Agency (NSA) and the Central Intelligence Agency (CIA), he encountered progressively disconcerting revelations about the extent and implications of mass surveillance programs. His participation in these operations exposed him to the intricate web of data collection, analysis, and monitoring that burgeoned under the auspices of national security and counterterrorism efforts.

The realization that both domestic and global communications were being indiscriminately swept up in the dragnet of surveillance activities began to sow seeds of apprehension in Snowden's mind. Witnessing the accumulation of vast troves of personal information, including digital communications, browsing habits, and metadata, triggered a deep sense of moral disquiet within him. The principles of privacy, civil liberties, and individual freedom, which form the bedrock of democratic society, clashed starkly with the pervasive scope of the surveillance apparatus he was part of.

Furthermore, as Snowden familiarized himself with the technical intricacies and capabilities of the surveillance systems, he became acutely cognizant of the potential for abuse and overreach. The unchecked power wielded by agencies in their pursuit of unchecked access and control over private communications and personal data served as a catalyst for disillusionment. This growing disenchantment with the pervasive surveillance culture set the stage for a profound shift in Snowden's perspective and ultimately propelled him down the path of whistleblowing.

Instead of embracing the status quo, Snowden grappled with ethical conflicts and moral imperatives, grappling with the clash between duty, loyalty, and integrity. His exposure to the inner workings and motivations behind the surveillance edifice ignited a fervent desire to challenge the encroachment on fundamental human rights and liberties. This internal turmoil forged a resolute determination to act, setting the stage for the fateful choices that would redefine Edward Snowden's trajectory and infiltrate the very fabric of global discourse surrounding privacy, security, and government transparency.

Key Influence and Decision Catalysts

In the pivotal phase of Edward Snowden's life, various key influences and catalysts converged to shape his monumental decision to blow the whistle on surveillance practices. Firstly, Snowden's encounters with whistleblowers and privacy advocates within and outside the intelligence community heightened his awareness of the ethical implications of mass surveillance. These interactions provided him with a nuanced understanding of the potential impacts of unchecked government surveillance on individual rights and civil liberties. Additionally, the revelations and controversies surrounding government programs such as PRISM and Boundless Informant deeply impacted Snowden's perception of the moral imperative to act. The accumulation of these experiences and encounters sowed the seeds of discontent that would eventually germinate into his decisive stance. Moreover, the mentorship and guidance from seasoned privacy advocates and legal experts played a crucial role in refining Snowden's critical thinking and fortifying his moral compass. These mentors imparted invaluable insights into the complex web of legal, ethical, and moral considerations surrounding whistleblowing, further crystallizing his resolve to take a stand. Furthermore, Snowden's introspective contemplation and self-assessment sessions, facilitated by journaling and deep reflection, served as a crucible for distilling his burgeoning concerns into a clarion call for action. This process allowed him to reconcile personal ethics with professional obligations, leading to the crystallization of his decision to reveal classified information. Lastly, the culmination of these influences and personal convictions coalesced into a watershed moment, as Snowden found himself standing on the precipice of history. With unwavering determination and a profound sense of duty, he stood ready to make an irreversible choice that would forever alter the global discourse on privacy, security, and individual freedom.

Conclusion: On the Brink of a Monumental Decision

As Edward Snowden found himself at the crossroads of his conscience and duty, he grappled with the unsettling realization that the systems he had dedicated himself to were being used in ways he could no longer condone. The culmination of experiences, encounters, and self-reflection had brought him to a defining moment - one that would shape the course of his life and reverberate across the global stage. Courage intertwined with concern as he pondered the weight of his decision, acutely aware of the seismic impact it would unleash. His resolve was cemented not by recklessness, but by an unwavering commitment to transparency and the preservation of civil liberties. It was in this introspective state that Snowden resolved to embark on a path that would radically alter his fate and ignite a paradigm shift in the world's understanding of surveillance, privacy, and government accountability. The profound gravity of his imminent actions bore upon him as he recognized the inevitability of sacrifices and the ramifications that would ensue from his unwavering determination to uphold the principles he held dear. With meticulous care and thorough contemplation, he meticulously charted the unfathomably consequential course ahead, propelled by an unyielding ethical compass that impelled him to navigate uncharted waters despite the harrowing uncertainties lurking on the horizon. The stark reality was that any retreat from this juncture would entail compromising his integrity and betraying the very ideals that had guided his journey thus far. As Snowden stood at the precipice of profound metamorphosis, he harbored no illusions about the long and arduous road that lay ahead. Nevertheless, driven by an unassailable pursuit of righteousness and the unwavering conviction that his actions were indispensable for the greater good, he steeled himself to confront the abyss that yawned before him. In the throes of this pivotal conclusion, an indomitable spirit was kindled within him, fueling a fierce determination to champion truth and accountability. And so, with resolute clarity and a steadfast commitment to his principles, Edward Snowden poised himself to irrevocably alter the landscape of global surveillance, permeating the ethos of contemporary society with an indelible legacy that transcended the confines of time.

3

The Decision

The Precipice of Change

Edward Snowden found himself on the precipice of change, a place that demanded unwavering courage and unyielding resolve. As he carefully navigated the corridors of power within the National Security Agency (NSA), his keen sense of duty was constantly pitted against the growing moral dilemmas that plagued his conscience. The weight of his responsibilities at NSA, coupled with the escalating realization of the extensive surveillance programs being operated, had cast a profound shadow over his mental and emotional state. It was amidst this turbulent backdrop that Snowden grappled with the profound complexity of his position, feeling the inexorable pull towards a pivotal decision that would ultimately alter the course of his life and reverberate through the annals of history.

Snowden's Role and Responsibilities at NSA

Edward Snowden began his journey into the world of intelligence and surveillance in 2006 when he joined the Central Intelligence Agency (CIA) as a technical expert. His exceptional aptitude in technology and his unwavering commitment to national security were quickly recognized, leading to his subsequent employment with the National Security Agency (NSA). Here, Snowden undertook various roles primarily focused on cybersecurity and infrastructure maintenance within the agency. As a contractor for the NSA through Booz Allen Hamilton, he was entrusted with high-level responsibilities involving the analysis and enhancement of digital security systems, giving him access to a wealth of classified information. Snowden's reputation as a proficient and dedicated analyst continued to flourish throughout his tenure at the NSA, solidifying his position as an essential asset in safeguarding the nation's cyber assets.

The Rise of Surveillance Concerns

As technology rapidly advanced in the digital age, so did the capabilities of surveillance. The post-9/11 era saw a significant increase in government-led surveillance programs, justified under the guise of national security. However, as these initiatives expanded, so too did concerns over the potential infringement on civil liberties and privacy rights. Snowden's tenure at the NSA coincided with a period when public unease about mass surveillance was mounting. The widespread adoption of digital communication platforms and smart devices meant that individuals' private data could be collected and analyzed on an unprecedented scale. This pervasive monitoring extended not only to potential threats but also encompassed vast swaths of innocent citizens. The revelation of programs like PRISM shed light on the scope and reach of these surveillance activities, sparking widespread unease and moral questioning. The evolving landscape of surveillance raised critical ethical and legal questions regarding the balance between security imperatives and the right to privacy. With the escalation of these concerns, Snowden found himself in a unique position to witness firsthand the increasingly intrusive nature of surveillance practices. The growing disconnect between the stated goals of these programs and their actual impact fueled a sense of moral obligation within him, precipitating a pivotal internal struggle. His experiences within the system would ultimately propel him to make an extraordinary decision that would reverberate across the globe.

Ethical Dilemmas Faced by Snowden

Within the complex web of modern surveillance practices, Edward Snowden found himself grappling with a myriad of ethical dilemmas that would ultimately shape the trajectory of his life. As he delved deeper into the inner workings of the National Security Agency (NSA), Snowden was confronted with the ethical implications of mass data collection and indiscriminate monitoring of global communications. His role as a contractor for the NSA necessitated an unwavering commitment to upholding national security, yet the ethical considerations surrounding individual privacy and civil liberties weighed heavily on his conscience.

Snowden's ethical dilemma extended beyond theoretical contemplation; it permeated his daily responsibilities and interactions within the secretive world of intelligence gathering. The tension between loyalty to the agency and fidelity to broader ethical principles became increasingly pronounced as Snowden grappled with the moral implications of his work. This internal conflict culminated in a profound realization - the realization that remaining silent would make him complicit in the perpetuation of a surveillance apparatus that he deemed to be fundamentally at odds with democratic values.

Furthermore, Snowden's ethical compass was further challenged by the realization that the scope and scale of surveillance activities far surpassed the public's awareness. This incongruence between public perception and the clandestine realities of state-sponsored surveillance raised critical questions about transparency, accountability, and the ethical obligations of those entrusted with wielding unparalleled technological power.

As Snowden navigated this ethical quagmire, he found himself forced to confront uncomfortable truths about the extent of government overreach and the erosion of privacy rights. The pervasive nature of the surveillance state, coupled with the lack of meaningful over-sight, presented a stark ethical quandary that demanded unwavering introspection and courage. Snowden's journey towards ethical clarity was fraught with uncertainties, personal sacrifices, and the relentless pursuit of alignment between his actions and his moral convictions.

Ultimately, Snowden's ethical dilemmas underscored the profound struggle between institutional allegiances and the ethical imperative to safeguard individual liberties. It was within the crucible of these dilemmas that Snowden's path towards becoming a whistleblower began to take shape, heralding a seismic shift in the landscape of international discourse on privacy, surveillance, and ethics.

Key Incidents Influencing the Decision

In the lead-up to his pivotal decision to blow the whistle on the NSA's clandestine surveillance programs, Edward Snowden found him-self immersed in a series of incidents that would forever shape his ethical outlook and drive him toward a fateful choice. As he delved deeper into the inner workings of the intelligence community, Snowden encountered numerous instances that rocked his belief in the morality and legality of the programs he was involved with. The first significant incident occurred when he stumbled upon evidence of warrantless wiretapping of US citizens, which sparked an internal conflict as he grappled with the implications of such pervasive intrusions on privacy and civil liberties. This revelation sowed the seeds of doubt in Snow-den's mind, laying the groundwork for the soul-searching that would subsequently unfold. Another formative incident transpired when he became privy to the extent of international surveillance activities by American agencies, fueling his growing unease and moral qualms about the global ramifications of such far-reaching operations. These revelations fueled Snowden's burgeoning sense of disillusionment and catalyzed a period of intense introspection, during which he mulled over the ethical weight of remaining silent versus exposing these en-croachments. Additionally, an encounter with fellow employees who expressed discomfort with the unchecked power wielded by the NSA solidified Snowden's growing conviction that action needed to be taken. Through these key incidents, Snowden's ethical resolve was steadily reinforced, pushing him closer to the precipice of disclosure, and setting the stage for the monumental decision that would reverberate globally.

Consultations and Contemplations

After experiencing the weight of the information he held, Edward Snowden sought guidance and input from trusted colleagues and confidants. These consultations served as a platform for deep reflection, allowing him to gain diverse perspectives on the potential ramifications of his intended actions. It became evident that this decision was not one to be made lightly, but rather with a thorough understanding of the impact it would have on global surveillance practices and the implications for international relations.

The contemplations that followed were marked by intense introspection coupled with an acute awareness of the ethical obligations inherent in his role. Snowden grappled with the tension between his allegiance to the state and his duty to the public. The recognition of the delicate balance between patriotism and the greater good weighed heavily on his conscience, driving him towards a path fraught with uncertainty yet emboldened by a profound sense of moral responsibility.

As he contemplated the gravity of his potential actions, Snowden delved into the annals of history to draw guidance from past instances of whistleblowing and the resulting societal impacts. This retrospective analysis enriched his understanding of the broader implications, reinforcing the magnitude of the decision confronting him. His contemplations spanned not only the immediate consequences within his professional sphere but also the broader implications for civil liberties, privacy rights, and democratic values.

The prospect of becoming a whistleblower prompted a meticulous consideration of the fallout that would ensue, both personally and professionally. Snowden painstakingly analyzed the potential repercussions, exploring the legal and political landscapes in which his disclosures would resonate. The weighing of risks against the perceived benefits underscored the depth of thought that underpinned his eventual course of action.

In his consultations and contemplations, Snowden navigated a labyrinth of ethical, moral, and practical considerations, ultimately emerging with a resolute understanding of the imperative need to act in the face of pervasive surveillance practices that encroached upon individual liberties. Through intellectual rigor and unwavering commitment to principled decision-making, Snowden honed his resolve, paving the way for the pivotal turning point in his journey toward becoming a whistleblower.

The Turning Point: Deciding to Act

Edward Snowden stood at a crossroads, faced with the weight of his decisions and the knowledge that he was about to embark on a path with irreversible consequences. The culmination of consultations and contemplations had brought him to this pivotal moment—the threshold of disclosing classified information to the world. Every step towards this juncture had been deliberate and weighed against the potential fallout and the greater good.

As Snowden meticulously assessed the implications of his actions, the gravity of the situation was undeniable. He grappled with ethical dilemmas, questioning the balance between loyalty to the government and duty to the public. The persistent erosion of privacy rights and the accumulating evidence of mass surveillance were catalysts for introspection, compelling Snowden to confront the moral imperative of his position within the National Security Agency (NSA).

Amidst these profound reckonings, Snowden sought counsel from trusted colleagues and individuals well-versed in matters of government transparency and civil liberties. He deliberated over the broader societal impact of his potential disclosures and sought to align his actions with a conviction deeply rooted in concerns for the fundamental rights of citizens.

The turning point came through a series of defining moments that crystallized Snowden's resolve. Instances of systemic abuse and unchecked power within the surveillance apparatus served as a clarion call, propelling him towards a concrete decision to act. With unwavering determination, Snowden committed to the monumental task of preparing for disclosures that would ignite global discourse and prompt unprecedented introspection within the realms of governance and individual freedoms.

Preparation for disclosures involved meticulous planning to ensure that the revelations would be conveyed in a manner that prioritized truth, transparency, and the protection of privacy. Snowden understood the weight of the impending repercussions and took meticulous measures to safeguard the integrity of the information while aiming to minimize collateral damage. As the pivotal moment drew nearer, the enormity of the decision weighed heavily on his conscience, yet strengthened his commitment to the principles that propelled him forward.

The turning point marked an unyielding affirmation of conscience, as Edward Snowden poised himself to challenge the status quo and advocate for a society founded on the bedrock of informed consent and constitutional rights. It represented the culmination of a journey punctuated by ethical discernment, introspection, and a resolute dedication to instigating change—ushering in an era where the voice of one individual could catalyze global reform and foster collective awareness.

Preparation for Disclosures

As Edward Snowden made the pivotal decision to act, meticulous preparation became crucial. In the period leading up to the disclosures, Snowden undertook a methodical approach to ensure that the critical information he intended to reveal was safeguarded, organized, and disseminated effectively. This phase involved meticulous planning, deliberation, and strategic execution of his intentions. Snowden's background as a highly competent IT professional equipped him with the technical proficiency required to prepare the vast trove of classified documents for dissemination. He meticulously collated and cataloged evidence of mass surveillance programs, recognizing that presenting a cogent narrative was essential in capturing global attention and credibility. The intricate process of preparing the disclosures necessitated thorough consideration of potential consequences on both personal and geopolitical levels. During this time, Snowden grappled with the weight of the responsibility he bore, mindful of the impact his actions would have on his own life and that of numerous individuals and institutions. While he felt compelled by a deep sense of duty, the enormity of the situation demanded unwavering composure and clear-headed resolve. Additionally, Snowden recognized the need to fortify his own defenses against anticipated reprisals and legal actions. This entailed meticulous contingency planning, including establishing communication channels with journalists and potential legal advisors in anticipation of the aftermath of his disclosures. The period preceding the revelations thus saw Snowden methodically readying himself for the complex web of reactions and implications that would inevitably ensue. In balancing the imperative to disclose vital information against potential ramifications, the decisions and preparations undertaken during this phase played a fundamental role in shaping the course of history.

Potential Risks and Consequences Considered

Edward Snowden's decision to become a whistleblower was not made lightly. In contemplating the potential risks and consequences of his actions, he faced an array of profound ethical and practical considerations. As he internally debated the necessity of his disclosures, Snowden meticulously weighed the potential ramifications that would inevitably ensue from his revelation of classified information. Among the foremost concerns were the serious legal repercussions he would face for violating the Espionage Act and potentially facing charges of treason or espionage.

Moreover, there was a deep understanding of the personal costs associated with exposing government secrets. Recognizing that his life would forever be altered, Snowden grappled with the knowledge that he would likely never be able to return to the United States and would endure a life of exile. His decision to reveal state secrets also exposed him to the risk of arrest or even assassination, as he became a target of powerful organizations deeply invested in maintaining the status quo.

Snowden knew that his actions would have far-reaching implications not only for himself, but also for those closest to him. The potential collateral damage to his family and loved ones weighed heavily on his mind, as he contemplated the repercussions they could face due to his whistleblowing. Additionally, considering the broader impact on diplomatic relations and international security, Snowden evaluated the potential disruption to global stability and the strain it could place on alliances between nations.

As Snowden delved into the complexities of the repercussions, he understood that the nature of his disclosures could result in profound shifts in public opinion, polarizing society and triggering extensive debate. The implications for national security and the surveillance apparatus could be seismic, with unforeseen impacts resonating throughout the world. Furthermore, he recognized the daunting challenge of managing the media storm that would inevitably follow, thrusting him into an unforgiving spotlight and subjecting him to intense scrutiny.

Ultimately, the intricacies and enormity of the risks and consequences weighed heavily on Snowden as he navigated the pivotal juncture at which he found himself. His resolve to confront these potential outcomes demonstrated tremendous courage and conviction, cementing his position as a historical figure whose choices reverberated globally.

Conclusion: The Resolve to Become a Whistleblower

After meticulous contemplation and weighing the potential risks and consequences associated with his decision, Edward Snowden arrived at a pivotal moment that would forever alter the trajectory of his life. With the knowledge of the far-reaching implications of his actions, Snowden exhibited unparalleled resolve as he committed to becoming a whistleblower. This resolution stemmed from a deeply ingrained sense of duty and an unwavering commitment to individual privacy, civil liberties, and the ethical responsibilities of those entrusted with classified information. Snowden's resolve to take on the mantle of a whistleblower was rooted in a genuine belief that the public had a right to be aware of the extensive surveillance activities being conducted by government agencies, a fact that had been concealed from the citizenry. As he contemplated the decision, it became increasingly evident to Snowden that the magnitude of the information he possessed necessitated exposure in service of greater public awareness and accountability. Despite acknowledging the potential personal repercussions that awaited him, such as legal ramifications, scrutiny, and enduring exile, Snowden's conviction remained unyielding. This unshakeable determination manifested in meticulous preparatory measures undertaken to ensure the responsible and secure disclosure of the classified information. As Snowden's moral compass guided him towards this unprecedented course of action, he endeavored to meticulously weigh the potential benefits of disclosure against the foreseeable adversities. The fundamental nature of his resolve lay in the unwavering belief that the public deserved to be made cognizant of the pervasive surveillance practices that encroached upon their civil liberties. Snowden's steadfastness in embracing the role of a whistleblower serves as a testament to his unwavering commitment to moral integrity and the principles of transparency and accountability. It underscores the gravity of the internal conflict and ethical dilemmas confronted by individuals entrusted with sensitive information and further underscores the profound implications of their decisions. Ultimately, the resolve to become a whistleblower was a profound demonstration of courage, conscience, and the unyielding pursuit of truth, foundations upon which Edward Snowden would build his enduring legacy.

4

Crossing the Threshold: From Analyst to Whistleblower

Setting the Stage

Edward Snowden's journey from an analyst within the National Security Agency (NSA) to becoming one of the most consequential whistleblowers in modern history marks a pivotal moment in the intersection of government surveillance, privacy rights, and individual conscience. To understand this transformation, it is imperative to delve into Snowden's initial role at the NSA, embedded within the complex web of intelligence gathering and analysis. As an NSA contractor employed by various firms, Snowden gained access to vast troves of classified information, allowing him to observe the inner workings of the U.S. intelligence apparatus. Within this context, he encountered a landscape characterized by unprecedented levels of domestic and global surveillance, powered by advanced technologies and underpinned by legal frameworks that raised profound ethical questions. As we explore Snowden's role at the NSA, we are compelled to examine how his involvement in these operations ignited a process of moral discernment and personal evolution. This introspective exploration will shed light on the catalysts that ultimately led Snowden to make the fateful decision to expose the extent of clandestine government programs, forever altering the discourse on privacy, security, and state accountability.

Snowden's Role at the NSA

Edward Snowden's role at the NSA was integral to understanding the extent of government surveillance and the ethical dilemmas he faced. As a contractor for the NSA, Snowden was entrusted with handling a vast amount of classified information. His job as a systems administrator granted him access to highly sensitive data, offering a unique vantage point on the inner workings of surveillance programs. This level of access allowed Snowden to witness firsthand the magnitude of the information being collected, as well as the potential consequences for individual privacy and civil liberties.

In his capacity at the NSA, Snowden worked within the infrastructure that enabled the agency to collect and analyze communication data on an unprecedented scale. His technical expertise and deep understanding of the surveillance systems provided him with a comprehensive view of the capabilities and reach of the agency's operations. Through his work, Snowden became increasingly aware of the ethical implications of the mass surveillance being conducted, grappling with the moral responsibility that came with his insider knowledge.

Snowden's pivotal role in maintaining and troubleshooting the surveillance infrastructure gave him insight into the breadth and depth of the programs. It was within this context that he began to question the morality and legality of the practices he was enabling. The more he delved into the inner workings of the NSA, the more conflicted he became about the implications of the agency's activities on a global scale.

At the heart of these revelations was Snowden's realization that the surveillance mechanisms he was deeply involved in threatened the fundamental rights and freedoms of individuals worldwide. This awareness placed him at a crossroads, as he grappled with the ethical considerations of loyalty to the agency versus the duty to uphold the principles of privacy and democracy. Snowden's evolving understanding of the profound impact of his role at the NSA would ultimately shape the trajectory of his future actions, leading to a decision that would reverberate globally.

Turning Points: Key Events Leading to Disclosure

Edward Snowden's decision to become a whistleblower and disclose classified information was not impulsive; it was the culmination of a series of significant events that led him to a pivotal moment in his career and personal ethics. One of the crucial turning points was his increasing disillusionment with the practices and policies he encountered during his time at the National Security Agency (NSA). As a former NSA contractor, Snowden became privy to extensive surveillance programs that he found deeply troubling. The realization that the NSA was engaged in widespread and indiscriminate data collection on both domestic and international targets served as a catalyst for his eventual actions. This awakening to the extent of government overreach fundamentally shook Snowden's trust in the system he had sworn to serve and protect. Another pivotal event was witnessing the erosion of privacy rights and civil liberties amidst the growing technological capabilities for mass surveillance. Snowden grappled with the inherent tension between national security imperatives and individual freedoms. The gravity of this ethical dilemma weighed heavily on him as he considered the potential consequences of coming forward with his concerns. Furthermore, Snowden's interactions with colleagues and superiors at the NSA contributed to his evolving perspective. He sought guidance from within the organization, only to encounter resistance and dismissal of his apprehensions. This internal friction amplified his sense of isolation and reinforced the growing belief that meaningful change could only occur through external disclosure. Throughout this period, Snowden underwent a profound internal struggle, torn between loyalty to his duty and allegiance to his conscience. Each of these turning points incrementally shaped his path towards becoming one of the most influential whistleblowers in modern history.

Moral and Ethical Considerations

Edward Snowden's decision to leak sensitive information raised profound moral and ethical considerations that continue to reverberate throughout the global community. At the crux of this dilemma are the fundamental principles of loyalty to one's organization versus loyalty to the public good, as well as the responsibility of upholding constitutional rights. Snowden's actions force us to reevaluate the balance between national security and individual privacy, and whether the means of surveillance justified the ends. This ethical quandary extends beyond Snowden himself, sparking debates on the role of whistleblowers in modern society and the obligations of individuals with access to classified information. It calls into question the accountability of government agencies and the extent to which citizens can trust their elected officials to act in their best interests. Additionally, considerations of international relations and potential impacts on diplomatic ties further complicate the ethical landscape. Furthermore, the repercussions of Snowden's actions have influenced how organizations approach internal dissent and the handling of confidential data. The underlying ethical tensions highlight the complex interplay between personal conscience, professional duty, and the broader social contract. Deeper reflection is required to navigate these intricate dilemmas, shaping the ongoing discourse on the role of transparency, accountability, and conscience in democratic societies.

The Mechanism of Leaking Sensitive Information

Leaking sensitive information is a complex and delicate process that demands meticulous planning and careful execution. Snowden's decision to act as a whistleblower was not a hasty or impulsive one, but rather a calculated and methodical step that required an intricate understanding of the mechanisms involved in leaking classified data. The process of leaking sensitive information begins with a comprehensive assessment of the material at hand. This involves identifying the nature and scope of the information, as well as evaluating its potential impact upon disclosure. Further considerations include the potential legal repercussions, ethical obligations, and the broader societal implications of such an action. Once the decision to proceed is made, the whistleblower must devise a strategy for accessing and extracting the sensitive data without raising suspicion. This often involves navigating elaborate security protocols and circumventing layers of institutional safeguards. Additionally, the whistleblower must consider the means through which the leaked information will be disseminated to the public or relevant authorities. Choosing the appropriate channels for disclosure is pivotal, as it directly influences the credibility and impact of the revelations. The strategic release of information requires careful coordination and collaboration with trustworthy individuals or entities capable of amplifying the message while ensuring the safety and anonymity of the whistleblower. It also involves meticulous consideration of timing, ensuring that the disclosures are made at a juncture that maximizes their resonance and potential for effecting change. Furthermore, the mechanism of leaking sensitive information entails post-disclosure measures to mitigate the risks faced by the whistleblower. This may involve seeking legal protection, asylum, or advocacy from international human rights organizations. Such measures are crucial in safeguarding the individual's wellbeing and ensuring that the disclosures catalyze constructive dialogue and reform, rather than subjecting the whistleblower to undue harm or persecution. As such, the mechanism of leaking sensitive information is a multifaceted and intricate process that demands a deep comprehension of the legal, ethical, and logistical dimensions inherent in whistleblowing.

Breaking Silence: The Decision to Act

Edward Snowden faced a formidable ethical dilemma when he made the decision to disclose sensitive government information. This momentous choice was not born out of recklessness, but from a deeply held conviction that the public had a right to know about the extent and implications of mass surveillance programs. The decision to act required careful consideration of the potential consequences, both personal and global.

Snowden recognized the gravity of his actions and understood the immense responsibility that came with revealing classified data. His contemplation delved into the delicate balance between loyalty to the government and loyalty to the citizens whose privacy he sought to protect. The weight of this decision extended beyond personal concerns, as Snowden grappled with the far-reaching impact his disclosure could have on national security, diplomatic relations, and individual freedoms.

In reaching his decision, Snowden meticulously evaluated the legal and ethical implications of his actions, seeking counsel from trusted colleagues and mentors. He engaged in introspection, questioning the moral imperative to adhere to unjust laws versus the obligation to expose systemic injustices. The internal turmoil that preceded his revelation underscored the magnitude of the choice before him—the choice to break silence and confront the covert nature of pervasive surveillance.

Snowden's deliberation was driven by a desire to spark a crucial conversation about transparency, accountability, and the proper use of state power. The significance of this pivotal moment in Snowden's journey lies in the profound realization that one individual's decision to act can galvanize transformative change at a societal level. The repercussions of this decision reverberated across the globe and initiated widespread scrutiny of surveillance practices, provoking discourse about civil liberties, privacy rights, and governmental oversight.

The decision to blow the whistle marked a definitive turning point in Snowden's life, propelling him into a tumultuous landscape fraught with legal battles, international fugitive status, and enduring exile. Yet, it also illuminated the unwavering commitment to principles of justice and democratic governance that underpinned his resolve. Snowden's decision to act embodied the ethos of civic responsibility and heralded an era of heightened awareness regarding the implications of digital privacy in the 21st century.

Relationships in Secret

In delving into the intricate world of intelligence agencies, it becomes apparent that relationships maintained within these organizations are often shrouded in secrecy. Edward Snowden's position as an Intelligence Analyst at the NSA required him to navigate a complex web of professional interactions that were heavily governed by confidentiality and trust. The connections Snowden forged with colleagues and superiors were steeped in clandestine nature due to the sensitive nature of the information they handled. Within the confines of this covert environment, Snowden's relationships were built on shared responsibilities, mutual dependencies, and strict hierarchies. The dynamics of these relationships, embedded in the secrecy of the intelligence community, played a pivotal role in shaping Snowden's eventual course of action. Furthermore, the element of secrecy in these relationships intensifies the pressure and ethical dilemmas faced by individuals like Snowden. The inherent tension between maintaining allegiance to one's organization and adhering to personal principles is magnified within these discreet relationships. The complexities of such secretive professional connections created significant internal conflicts for Snowden, ultimately culminating in his pivotal decision to blow the whistle on the NSA's controversial surveillance practices.

Data Transfer: The Practical Challenges

The process of transferring sensitive information from secure networks to the public domain is fraught with practical challenges. Edward Snowden, as a former NSA contractor, was acutely aware of the obstacles he would face in leaking classified data to journalists and the wider global audience. This section delves into the intricacies and hurdles inherent in the data transfer involved in Snowden's whistleblowing act. One of the primary challenges that Snowden encountered was the sheer amount of data he intended to disclose. Managing and extracting such vast volumes of information without raising suspicion or being detected posed a significant logistical obstacle. Additionally, ensuring the safe transmission of this data to journalists without interception by authorities required meticulous planning and technical expertise. The need for security measures to protect his identity and the integrity of the leaked documents added another layer of complexity to the data transfer process. Furthermore, Snowden had to navigate the labyrinth of encryption, secure communication channels, and anonymization techniques to safeguard the sensitive material during its transfer. These technical demands demanded a high level of proficiency and knowledge in cybersecurity and information technology. Moreover, the challenge extended beyond the mere act of transferring data. Snowden also had to grapple with the potential legal implications and the risk of being pursued by the US government, which necessitated strategic considerations throughout the transfer process. Balancing the urgency of disclosing the information with the requirement for meticulous execution placed immense pressure on Snowden as he orchestrated the transfer. This section will delineate the gripping details of Snowden's methodical approach to overcoming these practical challenges, shedding light on the intricate and high-stakes nature of his whistleblowing endeavor.

From Anonymity to Spotlight: Exposure Implications

The transition from anonymity to the spotlight is a pivotal moment for any whistleblower. For Edward Snowden, this journey into the public eye brought with it a whirlwind of exposure implications that reverberated on personal, professional, and global scales. As the world's attention turned towards him, Snowden found himself catapulted into an unfamiliar realm where every action and utterance carried immense weight. The sudden shift from a clandestine existence to being thrust under intense scrutiny reshaped his reality in profound ways.

Internally, the psychological toll of constant surveillance and the awareness of adversaries seeking retribution loomed large. Externally, media attention brought both support and vilification. It sparked debates surrounding the limits of government oversight, individual privacy, and national security. Snowden's revelations forced individuals, governments, and corporations to confront uncomfortable truths, igniting a reckoning with the implications of unchecked mass surveillance.

Furthermore, navigating the complexities of legal battles, asylum-seeking, and diplomatic negotiations added another layer of strain and complexity. Stripped of the sanctuary provided by anonymity, Snowden grappled with the repercussions of his choices and bore the weight of global attention. Amidst these trials, he became a symbol - a polarizing figure emblematic of the profound ethical quandaries faced by modern society.

As Snowden stepped into the limelight, his actions propelled him into uncharted territory, forever altering his relationship with privacy, security, and freedom. His journey from obscurity to prominence underscores the profound impact of exposure in the realm of whistle-blowing - shining a light on the sacrifices and tribulations inherent in challenging the status quo and daring to reveal uncomfortable truths.

Conclusion: Stepping Into a New Reality

Edward Snowden's journey from a low-profile analyst to a globally recognized whistleblower has thrust him into a new reality that has irrevocably altered the landscape of surveillance, privacy, and government accountability. As the dust settles on the exposure implications, it becomes evident that Snowden's actions were not just a tipping point in history but also a catalyst for international dialogue and legislative reform. In negotiating this new reality, both Snowden and the world he sought to impact must grapple with multifaceted repercussions.

The once-elusive veil of secrecy surrounding government surveillance has been lifted, leading society to confront uncomfortable truths about power, privacy, and democratic norms. This dramatic shift brings forth a multitude of challenges and opportunities, raising profound questions about the future of global governance, human rights, and technological ethics. Furthermore, in stepping into this new reality, Snowden's personal life has undergone a radical transformation. His choices have led to exile, legal battles, and a constant threat to his freedom. However, his unwavering commitment to transparency and moral duty has garnered him support as well as opposition from all corners of the globe. Snowden's newfound reality is one of paradoxes—having sacrificed his own liberty to defend the liberties of others. Despite the personal sacrifices and uncertainties, his actions have ignited unprecedented conversations and reforms across nations, prompting individuals and organizations to reevaluate their roles in upholding civil liberties and safeguarding data privacy. In parallel, the reverberations of Snowden's disclosures have injected momentum into the movement for digital rights advocacy, provoking the reassessment of surveillance laws and techno-political strategies. Moreover, his influence has transcended national borders, sparking debates on democratic principles, state oversight, and the limitations of executive power. As society grapples with these existential dilemmas, the legacy of Edward Snowden endures, resonating in ongoing efforts to adapt to this new reality and redefine the parameters of constitutional governance in an increasingly interconnected world.

5

The Whistleblower's Dilemma

Confronting the Moral Crossroads

Edward Snowden found himself at a pivotal moment in his life, faced with the weighty burden of knowledge that would ultimately alter the course of his personal and professional trajectory. The moral crossroads at which he stood loomed large, presenting him with an ethical quandary that transcended the boundaries of his role as an intelligence analyst. The revelation of classified information detailing expansive government surveillance programs placed Snowden in a precarious position, torn between allegiance to his country's security apparatus and his own growing unease with the implications of unchecked mass surveillance.

As he grappled with the enormity of the information he had access to, the gravity of Snowden's situation became increasingly palpable. His internal conflict intensified as he wrestled with the realization of the far-reaching implications of the clandestine activities he had become privy to. The sense of moral responsibility weighed heavily on him, prompting profound introspection and contemplation of the ethical ramifications of remaining silent in the face of pervasive infringements on privacy and civil liberties.

Various factors began to exert their influence on Snowden's decision-making process. On one hand, there was the specter of reprisal and professional censure should he choose to blow the whistle on the covert surveillance practices he had unearthed. The potential repercussions, both legally and socially, cast a daunting shadow over his deliberations, infusing his contemplations with a sense of foreboding uncertainty. Conversely, the nagging discomfort stemming from the moral imperative to bring to light the extent of government overreach continued to gnaw at Snowden's conscience, compelling him to confront the moral crossroads with unwavering resolve.

Amidst these tumultuous circumstances, Snowden found himself navigating a labyrinth of conflicting emotions and competing allegiances. The fervent desire to honor the oath of confidentiality that underpinned his work clashed with an increasingly fervent belief in the profound societal impact of exposing the invasive surveillance operations he had uncovered. This internal tension underscored the arduous nature of the decision-making process, underscoring the complex interplay of duty, morality, and personal conviction that permeated Snowden's predicament.

Against this backdrop, the juxtaposition of ethical imperatives and practical considerations ushered Snowden into a crucible of introspection. The delicate balance between professional obligation and individual conscience formed the crucible in which the contours of Snowden's character were tested, forging the path that would eventually lead to a decisive course of action. As he confronted the moral crossroads, the inexorable momentum of his evolving convictions propelled him toward a watershed moment echoing throughout the annals of modern history.

The Burden of Knowledge

The weight of knowledge can be both a blessing and a curse,

especially for individuals who find themselves at the precipice of disclosure. For whistleblowers like Edward Snowden, the burden of knowledge represents an internal struggle of epic proportions. The realization of possessing information that could potentially disrupt the status quo brings with it a profound sense of responsibility and duty. Embedded in this responsibility is the understanding that one's actions not only have the power to upend existing structures but also the potential to impact countless lives and shape the course of history. This burden of awareness can be all-consuming, compelling individuals to grapple with their conscience, values, and deepest convictions as they navigate the treacherous terrain of ethical decision-making. As Snowden wrestled with the extensive knowledge he possessed, he faced the overwhelming gravity of the choices before him, knowing full well that the path he chose would irreversibly alter his life and the world around him. The burden of knowledge is further compounded by intricate considerations of loyalty, patriotism, and the greater good. Whistleblowers often find themselves torn between their allegiance to their employers or government agencies and their perceived obligation to serve the public interest. This internal conflict generates palpable tension, forcing individuals to confront profound questions about where their true loyalties lie and what sacrifices they are willing to make in service of their principles. In Snowden's case, the burden of knowledge manifested as a complex web of moral and ethical quandaries, each strand pulling him in divergent directions and demanding careful contemplation. Furthermore, the burden of knowledge extends beyond personal considerations to encompass broader societal implications. Whistleblowers carry the weight of foreseeing potential repercussions on a global scale, cognizant of the seismic impact their revelations may generate. The grave nature of this responsibility underscores the magnitude of the burden that accompanies possessing sensitive and incendiary information. Ultimately, the burden of knowledge transcends mere awareness, evolving into a formidable force that shapes destinies and reshapes perceptions. For Edward Snowden, as for many whistleblowers, this burden became the crucible in which character, conviction, and consequences converged, propelling him towards an irrevocable choice that would echo across time.

Ethical Implications of Disclosure

Whistleblowing is a complex ethical decision burdened by profound moral considerations, especially when it involves exposing classified information to the public. The disclosure of sensitive material brings forth a myriad of ethical implications that must be carefully weighed and navigated. One of the primary ethical concerns surrounding disclosure is the potential harm it may inflict upon individuals, organizations, and even national security. While shedding light on unlawful activities or violations of privacy serves the common good, the repercussions of such revelations can be extensive and far-reaching.

Moreover, the act of disclosing classified information raises crucial questions about the whistleblower's duty to uphold the law and honor the trust placed in them. This ethical dilemma underscores the tension between loyalty to the government and the moral imperative to safeguard public welfare. Whistleblowers often grapple with conflicting loyalties, torn between their allegiance to the state and their commitment to truth and justice. The clash between these duties gives rise to a profound ethical struggle, wherein the individual must weigh the competing demands of institutional loyalty and societal accountability.

Additionally, ethical considerations in disclosure encompass the potential for breaching confidentiality agreements and violating legal mandates. Whistleblowers are faced with the daunting prospect of transgressing established norms and legal frameworks, raising critical questions about the boundaries of permissible dissent and the limits of societal obligation. A profound sense of responsibility underpins this decision, as whistleblowers shoulder the weight of holding powerful entities accountable while risking censure and persecution.

Furthermore, the ethical implications of disclosure extend to the broader impact on public trust and societal values. The decision to expose confidential information has the potential to either bolster or erode faith in institutions and democratic principles. It forces reflection on the values of transparency, accountability, and the ethical responsibilities of all citizens within a democratic society. This fundamental reevaluation of societal ethics underscores the transformative power of whistleblowing, shaping public discourse and collective perceptions of governance and corporate conduct.

Ethical deliberations surrounding disclosure demand a nuanced examination of the implications on individual lives, collective welfare, and the overarching fabric of society. They compel individuals to engage in profound introspection and moral scrutiny, resonating far beyond the immediate act of revealing classified information. Navigating these ethical considerations requires an acute awareness of the broader ramifications and a deep commitment to upholding the principles of integrity, justice, and societal well-being.

Analyzing Potential Harms and Benefits

Whistleblowing is a complex ethical and moral decision that requires careful consideration of the potential harms and benefits involved. As individuals grapple with the daunting prospect of exposing sensitive information, it becomes imperative to conduct a comprehensive analysis of the likely outcomes. This involves weighing the potential negative repercussions against the perceived benefits of disclosure. On one hand, whistleblowers must carefully assess the possible adverse effects on national security, diplomatic relations, and individual privacy rights. The exposure of classified information may also lead to legal ramifications, including prosecution and imprisonment. Moreover, there is a genuine concern for personal safety and security, as whistleblowers often face intimidation and retaliation from powerful entities.

Conversely, the potential benefits of whistleblowing cannot be overlooked. By shedding light on misconduct, corruption, or human rights violations, whistleblowers serve a critical role in upholding transparency, accountability, and the public interest. Their courageous actions can instigate positive systemic changes, leading to reforms in policies, practices, and institutions. Additionally, the act of whistleblowing may prompt meaningful public discourse and awareness, enabling informed debates regarding societal values and ethical standards. Ultimately, the careful analysis of potential harms and benefits serves as the linchpin of the whistleblower's dilemma, shaping their decision-making process and moral compass. It demands an unflinching commitment to upholding ethical principles amidst formidable challenges and uncharted territory.

Legal Risks of Whistleblowing

Whistleblowing is a courageous act fraught with legal complexities and potential repercussions. Before making the decision to disclose sensitive information, it is essential for whistleblowers to comprehend the legal risks associated with their actions. Engaging in whistleblowing can have far-reaching legal implications, often triggering various statutes and regulations that may lead to criminal charges or civil liabilities. Understanding the legal landscape is critical in assessing the potential impacts on personal freedom and professional standing.One of the primary legal considerations for whistleblowers is the possibility of facing charges under laws such as the Espionage Act or unauthorized disclosure of classified information. These laws impose severe penalties for individuals who divulge classified material, highlighting the gravity of the legal jeopardy whistleblowers face. In addition to federal statutes, whistleblowers may also encounter legal challenges related to breach of employment contracts, non-disclosure agreements, and intellectual property rights. These legal entanglements accentuate the need for whistleblowers to seek comprehensive legal counsel to navigate the intricate web of potential liabilities and defenses. Moreover, the prospect of civil litigation from aggrieved parties or government entities adds another layer of complexity to the legal framework. Whistleblowers must be prepared for the possibility of facing civil suits alleging defamation, breach of confidentiality, or other tortious conduct. Navigating these potential legal battles necessitates a thorough understanding of civil procedural rules and substantive defenses that can shield whistleblowers from unwarranted legal exposure.Furthermore, international implications can considerably augment the legal risks involved in whistleblowing, especially if the disclosed information implicates foreign governments, agencies, or entities. This introduces the specter of extradition treaties, international law, and diplomatic repercussions which may amplify the severity of legal consequences. As such, whistleblowers confronting this dilemma must grapple with the reality of multifaceted legal challenges that transcend domestic boundaries.Given the complex legal terrain associated with whistleblowing, prudent whistleblowers diligently assess the potential legal fallout, engage experienced legal advisors, and fortify their legal position before embarking on the precarious journey of exposing improprieties. While the decision to blow the whistle is fueled by moral imperatives, understanding the legal pitfalls is indispensable in mitigating risks and charting a path that aligns with ethical standards and legal boundaries.

Seeking Advice and Weighing Opinions

When facing the pivotal decision of whether to blow the whistle, seeking advice from trusted individuals becomes an essential aspect of mitigating the isolation and secrecy that often accompanies such a significant dilemma. While the burden of knowledge may feel isolating, it is crucial to seek diverse perspectives to weigh the implications of potential disclosure. Seeking advice provides an opportunity to gain insights from trusted mentors, colleagues, and legal experts, ensuring that all facets of the situation are comprehensively evaluated.

To effectively navigate the weight of this decision, whistleblowers must consider a wide array of opinions and advice, recognizing that each perspective contributes to a broader understanding of the complex ethical and legal considerations at play. Engaging in open, honest conversations with individuals who possess diverse expertise and experiences can aid in gaining a holistic understanding of the potential outcomes of their actions, allowing for a thoughtfully informed decision-making process. Furthermore, receiving guidance from legal professionals offers valuable insights into the potential ramifications of disclosing sensitive information, providing a clearer picture of the legal risks and implications associated with various courses of action.

Weighing these opinions requires objectivity and discernment, as conflicting advice may amplify the complexity of the decision. Whistle-blowers walking this challenging path must recognize that differing viewpoints stem from varied interpretations of the ethical, legal, and moral dimensions inherent in this predicament. This multifaceted counsel equips individuals with a more comprehensive understanding of the potential impacts of their choices, aiding in the formulation of a well-informed and morally conscious decision. However, navigating through differing opinions can also induce additional pressure and un-certainty, requiring individuals to maintain a steadfast focus on the core values guiding their integrity and sense of responsibility.

In conclusion, seeking advice and weighing opinions serves as a vital component in the whistleblower's journey, offering invaluable in-sights that contribute to a well-rounded assessment of the ethical, legal, and personal dimensions of the tumultuous decision at hand. The art of considering diverse perspectives and prudent counsel arms individuals with the necessary tools to make an informed and ethically grounded choice amidst the profound intricacies defining the whistleblower's dilemma.

Struggling with Isolation and Secrecy

Whistleblowers often find themselves confronted with the over-whelming weight of isolation and secrecy as they grapple with the decision to disclose sensitive information. This period is characterized by an intense sense of solitude, a feeling that one stands on the preci-pice of irreversible action with nobody to fully understand the gravity of the situation. The burden of maintaining secrecy, particularly in the face of a matter so profound, places a heavy toll on individuals who must navigate this turbulent terrain alone. In the absence of being able to confide in colleagues or loved ones, whistleblowers are frequently plagued by a profound sense of isolation, which can foster feelings of alienation and abandonment. This isolation is compounded by the necessity of keeping secrets from those closest to them, adding layers to the challenge of bearing the crucial choice they are carrying. The knowledge that disclosure could irreversibly alter their lives and the lives of others weighs heavily, further intensifying the internal struggle. Additionally, the anguish of not being able to share this knowledge with those they hold dear, for fear of the potential repercussions on both their own lives and the future trajectories of their relationships, adds to the emotional burden. Rationalizing the necessity of such isolation and managing the associated emotional distress requires resilience beyond measure. Despite navigating through this labyrinth of isolation, whistleblowers persevere by looking towards the greater impact their actions may have. They strive to uphold the principles that drive their mission and endeavor to shield loved ones from the harsh realities of their solitary struggle. Ultimately, as they navigate this tempest alone, their commitment to their cause and the greater good serves as a guiding beacon to weather the storm of isolation and secrecy.

Choosing the Path of Maximum Impact

Upon reaching the pivotal juncture of weighing the consequences against the significance of disclosure, Snowden found himself deeply entrenched in a labyrinth of conflicting considerations and ethical quandaries. Knowing that his actions would reverberate across the globe, he grappled with the weight of the knowledge he held and the profound impact it could have on society at large. Striving to balance the imperative of transparency with the potential fallout, he sought counsel from trusted confidants and experts in the field. As the gravity of his decision loomed ever closer, Snowden meticulously evaluated the various pathways before him, each carrying its own set of momentous implications. The desire to effect lasting change clashed with the sobering realization of the personal sacrifices that lay ahead.

Every step was fraught with the awareness that this irrevocable choice would reshape the course of his life. Amidst the seclusion and tension that enveloped him, Snowden relentlessly pursued a course of action that aligned with his unyielding commitment to the public good. Contemplating the far-reaching ramifications of his choices, he carefully steered towards the path that promised to yield maximal impact. Recognizing the inexorable nature of history in the making, he steeled himself for the tumultuous aftermath, resolute in his resolve to expose the truth. Embracing a sense of purpose that transcended personal concerns, Snowden made the defining pledge to uphold the highest ideals of justice and accountability. His unwavering determination propelled him towards the precipice of revelation, where the resonance of his actions would transcend the confines of individual fate and resonate throughout the annals of contemporary history.

Preparing for Personal and Professional Fallout

In the face of difficult decisions, preparation becomes paramount. As the whistleblower contemplates their impending disclosure, they must meticulously prepare for the personal and professional fallout that is almost certain to follow. This involves a deep introspection into the potential consequences, both on an individual level and within the broader context of their career and relationships.

First and foremost, the whistleblower must steel themselves for the emotional toll that their actions will likely exact. The prospect of facing public scrutiny, ostracization, and even legal repercussions can take a significant mental and emotional toll. It is crucial for the whistleblower to seek out a support network, whether it be trusted confidantes, legal counsel, or advocacy groups, to help navigate the turbulent waters ahead.

Simultaneously, the whistleblower must also brace themselves for the professional backlash that may ensue. Whistleblowing often leads to strained or severed professional relationships, as well as potential career setbacks. It is essential to craft a strategic plan for mitigating the impact on one's livelihood, possibly by seeking alternative employment opportunities or laying the groundwork for potential legal defense.

Moreover, in anticipating the fallout, the whistleblower must meticulously safeguard any evidence or documentation that supports their claims. This not only serves as a protective measure in the event of legal proceedings, but also bolsters the credibility of their disclosures. Careful consideration must be given to how this documentation is stored and shared, ensuring that it remains secure and accessible when needed most.

Another aspect that cannot be overlooked is the potential strain on personal relationships that might result from the whistleblower's decision. Family and friends may find themselves inadvertently embroiled in the controversy, leading to tension and conflict. Open and honest communication with loved ones, coupled with a willingness to address their concerns and fears, can help preserve these vital connections amid the turmoil.

Ultimately, the preparations for personal and professional fallout necessitate a meticulous and multi-faceted approach that safeguards the whistleblower's well-being while fortifying their position as they brace for the impact of their courageous decision.

The Final Decision: Compelling Reasons to Act

As the crescendo of internal conflict reaches its peak, the pivotal moment for action looms large. The whistleblower is acutely aware that the decision they are about to make will irrevocably alter the trajectory of their life. Numerous compelling reasons weigh on their conscience, urging them to act in the face of daunting adversity and uncertainty.

Foremost among these reasons is the deep-seated conviction that the public has a fundamental right to know about the pervasive surveillance practices that encroach upon their privacy and civil liberties. The whistleblower grapples with the moral imperative to serve the greater good by exposing the truth, acknowledging that failing to act would perpetuate the injustice and deception perpetrated against an unwitting populace. This profound sense of ethical responsibility serves as a bedrock for the decision-making process, driving the whistleblower to confront the formidable institutional forces that seek to shroud the truth in darkness.

Furthermore, the dire need for systemic reform propels the whistleblower towards taking decisive action. They recognize that the revelations brought to light have the potential to catalyze tangible changes in policy, governance, and oversight mechanisms. By daring to speak out, the whistleblower endeavors to trigger a seismic shift in societal consciousness, fostering a climate of accountability and transparency that demands redressal for overreaching surveillance and unchecked power.

Amidst this crucible of conflicting motivations and unwavering determination, the whistleblower draws strength from the harrowing accounts of individuals whose rights have been violated and freedoms curtailed under the cloak of clandestine surveillance programs. The human stories of those ensnared in the dragnet of mass data collection serve as a poignant reminder of the real-world consequences that underscore the urgency of exposing these abuses. It is this empathetic resonance that compels the whistleblower to cast aside personal trepidations in favor of championing the cause of the disenfranchised and vulnerable.

Navigating the intricate labyrinth of legal ramifications, the whistleblower grapples with the sobering realization that their actions may exact a heavy toll on their personal and professional well-being. Despite this daunting prospect, the unyielding resolve to confront the uncomfortable truths emboldens the whistleblower to surmount the paralyzing fear of reprisal, embracing the conviction that the pursuit of justice necessitates sacrifice and courage.

In this crucible of ethical, moral, and practical considerations, amidst the tumult of conflicting emotions and profound existential dilemmas, the whistleblower arrives at the inexorable conclusion—a decision shaped by the indomitable force of ethical duty, social responsibility, and unwavering commitment to truth and justice.

6

Confronting the Consequences

Initial Reactions and Retaliation

In the immediate aftermath of Edward Snowden's revelations, the U.S. government was engulfed in a whirlwind of responses, each reflecting the complexity of balancing security imperatives with the right to privacy. Government officials, including the President, emphasized the severity of the leaked information and condemned Snowden's actions as treasonous. The intelligence community underwent unprecedented scrutiny, with agencies such as the NSA facing intense backlash for their clandestine mass surveillance programs. This prompted a robust, albeit polarized, debate within political circles, as proponents of national security measures clashed with advocates of civil liberties in an ideological tug-of-war that reverberated across Capitol Hill.

In addition to public statements, the government's retaliation against Snowden was swift and comprehensive. The issuance of warrants for his arrest under the Espionage Act sent shockwaves through the international community and fueled an intricate legal battle that transcended domestic borders. Furthermore, the revocation of Snowden's passport and relentless pursuit for his extradition underscored the extent of the government's determination to bring him to justice, showcasing the depths of its resolve amidst one of the most significant intelligence breaches in modern history.

While the government's response aimed to contain the fallout and project authority, it also galvanized a groundswell of dissent from advocacy groups and privacy champions who decried the erosion of civil liberties. This culminated in legal and legislative challenges to the controversial surveillance practices brought to light by Snowden's disclosures, significantly reshaping the discourse surrounding the boundaries of state authority and personal privacy rights. Consequently, the aftermath of Snowden's revelations witnessed a seismic reconfiguration of the political landscape, pitting entrenched security paradigms against mounting calls for constitutional protections and individual freedoms.

Government Response: Security versus Privacy

The revelation of widespread surveillance by the government, as disclosed by Edward Snowden, triggered a monumental debate about the delicate balance between national security and individual privacy. The government response to these revelations was multifaceted, reflecting the complex interplay of interests at stake. On one hand, there was a palpable concern for preserving national security in an increasingly volatile global landscape. This prompted officials to emphasize the vital role of surveillance in safeguarding the populace from external threats, advocating that the collection of data was crucial for preempting potential acts of terrorism and maintaining state sovereignty.

However, this staunch stance on security was juxtaposed against the escalating apprehension surrounding the infringement upon personal privacy rights. Citizens and advocacy groups voiced profound unease about the extent of government intrusion into their private lives, contending that unchecked surveillance posed a significant threat to civil liberties and democratic values. The government found itself grappling with the imperative of assuaging public fears while upholding its narrative of security imperatives.

This quandary led to intricate policy deliberations and legislative initiatives aimed at recalibrating the boundaries between security imperatives and individual privacy rights. Heightened calls for transparency and mechanisms of oversight resonated across political arenas, as policymakers endeavored to restore public trust while reconciling the exigencies of security measures with constitutional protections. The intricacies of modern technology further compounded this conundrum, compelling lawmakers to confront the implications of technological advancements on surveillance capabilities and individual autonomy.

Various branches of the government engaged in protracted discourse over the requisite reforms to strike a sustainable equilibrium between security imperatives and privacy considerations. Specialized committees convened to assess the efficacy and legality of existing surveillance programs, while executive actors navigated the complexities of foreign diplomacy amidst the international fallout from Snowden's disclosures. Amidst this intricate dance of policy formulation, judicial bodies grappled with pivotal cases that tested the legal boundaries of surveillance practices, contributing to a landscape of evolving jurisprudence.

Ultimately, the government response to Snowden's revelations encapsulated a tempestuous interplay between the imperatives of safeguarding national security and the imperative of upholding individual privacy rights. It underscored the formidable challenges entailed in striking a harmonious balance between these ostensibly conflicting precepts, evoking a crucible of introspection and reform within the corridors of power.

Media Impact and Public Opinion

The media's coverage of Edward Snowden's revelations had an unprecedented impact on public opinion and discourse. As news of the leaked documents spread, it sparked intense debates and discussions on the role of government surveillance, individual privacy rights, and the ethics of whistleblowing. Media outlets around the world extensively covered the story, presenting varying perspectives on Snowden himself and the information he exposed. The reporting ranged from portraying him as a heroic whistleblower intent on exposing government overreach to depicting him as a treasonous traitor threatening national security.

Public opinion became polarized, with supporters lauding Snowden for his courage in standing up for civil liberties while detractors vilified him for endangering national security. The media's framing of the debate further fueled this divide, amplifying the emotive nature of the discourse. With each new revelation and development in the saga, media outlets provided extensive analysis and commentary, shaping the narrative around Snowden and the implications of his actions.

Additionally, the media's coverage not only elevated Snowden to international recognition but also brought discussions about surveillance and privacy into the mainstream consciousness. His disclosures prompted individuals to reevaluate their relationship with technology and raised pressing questions about the extent of government intrusion into personal communications and data. The dialogue spurred by the media coverage played a crucial role in fostering greater awareness and understanding of digital privacy among the general public.

Furthermore, the global media scrutiny exerted pressure on governments and intelligence agencies to address the concerns raised by Snowden's disclosures. It led to heightened transparency demands, calls for accountability, and the initiation of public inquiries into surveillance practices. The media's relentless spotlight on these issues spurred a reassessment of existing policies and instigated pivotal conversations at both national and international levels.

Ultimately, the media's profound influence in shaping public opinion and catalyzing societal reflection on surveillance and privacy rights marked a pivotal juncture in contemporary history. The symbiotic relationship between media coverage and public perception underscored the significant role of journalism in holding power to account and fostering informed civic discourse.

Legal Ramifications for Snowden

Edward Snowden's actions had immense legal ramifications, triggering a series of complex legal battles that reverberated across international borders. As his disclosures exposed the extent of government surveillance, they raised critical legal questions regarding privacy rights, government transparency, and national security. Upon releasing classified information to the media, Snowden faced charges under the Espionage Act in the United States. The legal framework surrounding whistleblowing, national security, and Freedom of Information Act (FOIA) came into sharp focus as the controversies unfolded. Governments worldwide were compelled to re-evaluate their legal procedures and responses to similar future cases.

Additionally, Snowden's revelations prompted widespread debate concerning the legitimacy and scope of government surveillance programs, leading to legal challenges against mass data collection practices and warrantless wiretapping. These legal battles ignited discussions about constitutional rights and the boundaries of governmental authority in the digital age. Legal experts, civil liberties advocates, and policymakers engaged in fervent debates about striking a balance between security imperatives and the protection of individual rights. The legal community witnessed unprecedented scrutiny of surveillance laws and judicial oversight mechanisms, which laid the groundwork for legislative reforms and heightened judicial review of intelligence activities.

Furthermore, the legal aftermath extended beyond domestic jurisdictions, prompting diplomatic tensions and legal conundrums in global relations. The extradition requests and asylum considerations brought international law and human rights treaties to the forefront. Countries found themselves grappling with the intricate web of extradition treaties, bilateral agreements, and asylum laws. At the crossroads of law and geopolitics, Snowden's case ignited multifaceted legal implications that transcended conventional legal boundaries. The legal ramifications of Snowden's actions initiated a paradigm shift in governmental transparency, national security discourse, and individual privacy protections, leaving an enduring legacy on the legal landscape.

Effects on Intelligence Community Practices

The revelations made by Edward Snowden had far-reaching consequences that permeated through the fabric of intelligence community practices, triggering a seismic shift in the way security and surveillance were conducted. The exposure of widespread, indiscriminate data collection programs sent shockwaves through the intelligence agencies worldwide, prompting rigorous reevaluation of their operational methodologies. As these agencies grappled with the fallout of Snowden's disclosures, they faced heightened public scrutiny, necessitating a delicate balance between national security imperatives and the protection of individual privacy rights. In response to the public outcry, intelligence communities were compelled to undertake comprehensive reviews of their surveillance techniques, leading to introspection and reforms in the pursuit of greater transparency and accountability.

Moreover, the Snowden revelations engendered a climate of increased caution within the intelligence community, fostering a culture of heightened vigilance to prevent further leaks and ensuring the safeguarding of sensitive information. The exposure of the inner workings of surveillance programs led to an era of tighter controls and enhanced compartmentalization, dictating a need for stricter oversight mechanisms and stringent protocols governing access to classified data. Consequently, intelligence agencies across the globe sought to fortify their internal security measures, implementing multifaceted strategies aimed at averting potential breaches and maintaining the confidentiality of their operations.

The impact of Snowden's disclosures also spurred an evolution in the landscape of intelligence gathering and analysis, as agencies adapted to navigate the evolving terrain of digital communication and technological advancements. Recognizing the vulnerabilities exposed by the leaks, intelligence communities embarked on modernization initiatives to bolster their capabilities in the face of emerging cyber threats, striving to strike a delicate equilibrium between harnessing technological innovations for effective intelligence gathering while respecting privacy and civil liberties. This transformative phase witnessed a paradigm shift in the approach to surveillance, emphasizing the ethical considerations and legal boundaries underpinning intelligence activities, culminating in a recalibration of the modus operandi of intelligence community practices.

Technological Companies' Standpoint

The revelations brought forth by Edward Snowden regarding the extensive surveillance programs conducted by government entities had a profound impact on technological companies, compelling them to re-evaluate their stance on user privacy and data protection. These companies found themselves at a crossroads, balancing the pressures from government agencies seeking access to user information for national security reasons against the growing demand for transparency and privacy from their user base.

First and foremost, the disclosure of mass data collection activities prompted a wave of concern among technology firms, as it fundamentally challenged the trust relationship between these companies and their users. The leaked documents revealed the extent to which government agencies were covertly accessing user data without clear oversight or legal consent, raising ethical and moral questions about the responsibility of technology companies to safeguard user privacy. This realization spurred internal discussions and public declarations from major technology players, many of whom publicly denounced the indiscriminate surveillance practices and advocated for stronger privacy protections.

Moreover, the technological landscape witnessed a shift in attitudes towards encryption, an essential tool in securing digital communications and protecting data from unauthorized access. In the wake of

Snowden's disclosures, there emerged a heightened emphasis on forti-fying encryption methods and implementing robust security measures to counteract potential government overreach. This shift was not merely confined to rhetoric; rather, prominent companies undertook proactive steps to bolster encryption standards and fortify the overall security infrastructure of their products and services, prioritizing user privacy in light of mounting concerns.

Furthermore, tech giants and start-ups alike began reassessing their cooperation with government data requests, demanding greater trans-parency in the surveillance-related demands imposed upon them. This push for transparency was propelled by a commitment to inform their users of any government data requests and legal obligations while concurrently advocating for reforms aimed at curtailing unchecked surveillance powers. In some instances, companies engaged in legal battles to challenge the secrecy surrounding government surveillance orders, signaling a willingness to contest overbroad or unconstitutional demands for user data.

In essence, the seismic shockwaves set off by Edward Snowden's disclosures compelled technological companies to rethink their role in safeguarding user privacy and digital rights. Their evolving stance represented a pivotal point in the larger discourse on surveillance and individual liberties, prompting a paradigmatic shift that underscored the imperative of upholding fundamental rights in an increasingly digitized world.

Reaction from Human Rights Organizations

The revelations made by Edward Snowden regarding the pervasive surveillance activities of government agencies sparked a firestorm of concern and criticism from human rights organizations around the world. These organizations, dedicated to upholding fundamental hu-man rights and protecting individuals from abuse of power, were quick to react to the implications of Snowden's disclosures. The exposed scope of mass data collection and monitoring raised serious ethical and legal questions for these organizations.

Human rights advocates decried the intrusiveness of mass surveillance as a violation of privacy rights enshrined in international law and constitutions of many nations. They argued that the indiscriminate gathering of communications data without justifiable cause represented an affront to the right to privacy, freedom of expression, and protection against arbitrary interference with one's personal life. Additionally, the potential for abuse of this vast trove of information underscored concerns about the erosion of civil liberties and the chilling effect on free speech and dissent.

Further, human rights organizations highlighted the disproportionate impact of mass surveillance on marginalized and vulnerable communities. The indiscriminate collection and surveillance of personal data could exacerbate existing inequalities and reinforce patterns of discrimination, posing a direct threat to the rights and well-being of minority groups, activists, journalists, and dissidents.

Moreover, the global nature of surveillance programs raised complex jurisdictional and sovereignty issues, prompting human rights organizations to call for greater transparency, oversight, and accountability in the practices of intelligence agencies. They emphasized the need for robust safeguards, independent judicial review, and clear limitations on surveillance activities to prevent abuse and protect individual rights.

In response to the revelations, these organizations actively engaged in public advocacy, litigation, and policy discourse to push for reforms, increased transparency, and stronger protections for privacy and free expression. Their efforts aimed to galvanize public awareness, shape public opinion, and influence legislative and regulatory action at national and international levels.

Ultimately, the reaction from human rights organizations served as a critical catalyst in elevating the public discourse on surveillance, forging alliances across civil society, and driving momentum for comprehensive reforms to safeguard fundamental rights in the digital age.

Impact on International Relations

The repercussions of Edward Snowden's revelations extended far beyond the borders of the United States, cascading into a global diplomatic maelstrom. The international community was thrown into disarray as governments grappled with the implications of the NSA's mass surveillance programs. At the heart of the matter lay profound concerns over sovereignty, trust, and mutual respect among nations.

In the immediate aftermath of the leaks, the diplomatic landscape underwent seismic shifts. Allies and foes alike found themselves re-evaluating their relationships with the U.S., questioning the integrity of intelligence-sharing agreements and alliances. Relations between the U.S. and certain countries were strained as accusations of espionage and breach of privacy reverberated across the globe. The revelations elicited strong reactions from governments, with some openly condemning the actions of the NSA while others wrestled with internal debates on the balance between national security and individual privacy.

Furthermore, the disclosures intensified existing tensions between the U.S. and other global powers, propelling discussions on cybersecurity, surveillance practices, and the protection of fundamental rights in the digital age to the forefront of international discourse. The fallout from Snowden's disclosures prompted an urgent reevaluation of the norms and protocols governing cyber espionage, igniting debates in multilateral forums and intergovernmental organizations such as the United Nations and the European Union. Consequently, international relations were marked by increased scrutiny, suspicion, and recalibration of foreign policies, with significant ramifications for diplomacy and global governance.

Moreover, the rifts caused by the surveillance revelations catalyzed shifts in geopolitical dynamics and reshaped collaboration on critical security matters. Countries faced dilemmas in reconciling their ties with the U.S. amidst mounting public outcry and pressure for transparency. Foreign leaders navigated the delicate balance between preserving vital partnerships and addressing domestic demands for accountability and

scrutiny. As a result, the landscape of international relations bore witness to tangible aftershocks, engendering enduring impacts on trust
and cooperation in an interconnected world.

The gravity of Snowden's disclosures also underscored the need
for transnational dialogues on digital privacy, surveillance oversight,
and the ethical boundaries of intelligence activities. These dialogues
precipitated efforts to establish common frameworks for upholding
privacy rights and regulating surveillance practices in a manner that
respects national sovereignty and individual liberties. Collaborative
initiatives emerged to foster consensus and solidarity among nations
seeking to address the complexities and moral imperatives inherent in
the cross-border dimensions of modern surveillance technologies. The
revelations ignited a collective call for greater transparency, accountability, and adherence to internationally recognized principles of human rights and democratic governance, spurring reshaped dynamics in
global engagement and diplomatic engagements around shared values
and interests.

Potential Amendments in Surveillance Laws

The revelations brought to light by Edward Snowden's disclosures
have catalyzed global discussions on the need for amendments in
surveillance laws. The pervasive nature of surveillance, as exposed
by the leaks, has raised concerns about the protection of individual
privacy and civil liberties. Governments around the world have faced
mounting pressure to reevaluate and potentially amend their existing
surveillance laws to strike a balance between security imperatives and
fundamental rights.

In the United States, the disclosures prompted significant legislative
and policy debates regarding the parameters of government surveillance. This led to the eventual passage of the USA Freedom Act in
2015, which sought to curtail the bulk collection of telecommunication
metadata by intelligence agencies and introduce enhanced transparency
and accountability measures. Additionally, ongoing legal battles and

advocacy efforts continue to shape the trajectory of surveillance law in the country.

Similarly, in the European Union, Snowden's revelations spurred profound reexaminations of data protection regulations and oversight mechanisms. The landmark ruling by the Court of Justice of the European Union in 2020 invalidated the EU-U.S. Privacy Shield framework, citing concerns over U.S. surveillance practices. This decision underscored the imperative for national and supranational entities to revisit frameworks governing transatlantic data transfers and strengthen safeguards against mass surveillance.

Beyond traditional legislative avenues, the evolving landscape of surveillance laws encompasses diverse dimensions, including jurisprudence, technological innovation, and international cooperation. Courts globally have grappled with pivotal cases that challenge the constitutionality and proportionality of mass surveillance programs. The intersection of law and technology presents a fertile ground for judicial interpretation and precedent-setting decisions that shape the contours of surveillance governance.

Furthermore, the growing consensus among technologists, privacy advocates, and legal scholars underscores the necessity for comprehensive legal reforms to address the proliferation of surveillance capabilities. Calls for robust encryption standards, stringent limitations on government access to private communications, and heightened judicial oversight have emerged as focal points in the discourse surrounding surveillance law amendments.

As the debate persists, a crucial consideration lies in striking an equilibrium that upholds national security obligations while safeguarding individual rights. The task of revising surveillance laws demands meticulous calibration to adapt to evolving threats, technological advancements, and societal expectations. The enduring legacy of Edward Snowden's revelations resides in its role as a catalyst for reinvigorated scrutiny and deliberation concerning the parameters and justifications of contemporary surveillance practices.

Snowden's Personal Consequences

Following the disclosure of classified information to the public, Edward Snowden faced an array of personal consequences that transcended the immediate impact on the global political stage. As a former contractor for the National Security Agency (NSA), his decision to reveal the extent of government surveillance programs led to a profound transformation in his personal life. Snowden's exposure of covert programs and his subsequent exile provoked a series of repercussions that profoundly shaped his day-to-day existence.

The path towards exile began with the revocation of Snowden's passport by the US government, leaving him stranded in transit at Moscow's Sheremetyevo Airport. This marked the inception of his asylum-seeking odyssey, as he remained confined within the airport's confines for over a month before ultimately being granted temporary asylum in Russia. This twist of fate initiated Snowden's unexpected residency in Russia, fueling widespread speculation about his potential motivations and affiliations.

While secluded in a foreign land, Snowden endured the psychological toll of isolation and separation from his homeland and loved ones. His personal relationships were irrevocably altered as he grappled with the ramifications of his actions. Motivated by a deep-seated belief in the ethical imperative to safeguard individual privacy and civil liberties, Snowden willingly sacrificed the comforts of his prior life in pursuit of his cause, testing the fortitude of his resilience amid the turmoil.

The legal labyrinth resulting from Snowden's disclosures underscored the complex entanglements he faced. Faced with espionage charges by the US government, his options for reintegration into society became inexorably limited. The specter of prosecution loomed over his every move, casting a pall over any conceivable return to the United States. Additionally, ongoing debates regarding his status as a whistleblower or traitor further complicated the prospects for any semblance of reprieve.

In the wake of his revelations, Snowden encountered a dichotomous response from the global community, with some hailing him as a hero while others condemned him as a traitor. The enduring discord surrounding his actions tested the foundation of his principles and instigated a sea change in public perception. Despite these adversities, Snowden remained resolute in his convictions, underscoring the unwavering resolve that propelled him to assume the mantle of a whistleblower despite the seismic aftershocks it unleashed upon his life.

The prospect of confronting personal consequences was intrinsic to Snowden's decision to disclose classified surveillance practices. His journey embodied a steadfast commitment to principle and spurred a confluence of personal tribulations, legal battles, and relentless scrutiny. Amidst this maelstrom, he emerged as an emblem of principled dissent, irrevocably altering the course of his own destiny while catalyzing a global discourse on the delicate balance between governmental authority and individual privacy.

7

Global Shockwaves: The International Response

Setting the Global Stage

At the time of Edward Snowden's revelations, the global context of privacy and surveillance was amid a profound paradigm shift. The interconnectedness of nations through advanced technology had drastically altered the traditional concepts of security, privacy, and intelligence gathering. Governments across the world were grappling with the unprecedented challenges presented by rapid technological advancements, raising critical questions about the balance between national security imperatives and individual privacy rights. This shifting landscape had laid the foundation for an era characterized by heightened debates on the ethical and legal implications of surveillance activities. In essence, the international community was at a crossroads, navigating the complexities of a digital age where information could be both empowering and perilous. The competing interests of security agencies, technology companies, and civil liberties advocates had woven a complex web that transcended borders and permeated the collective consciousness of societies worldwide. Against this backdrop, the disclosure of extensive surveillance programs by the U.S. National Security Agency sent shockwaves through diplomatic corridors, triggering multifaceted responses from governments around the globe. It prompted an urgent reevaluation of existing alliances, treaties, and norms, as states confronted the ramifications of mass surveillance on their own citizens and foreign entities. Understanding the global stage in which these events transpired is essential to grasping the depth of impact that Snowden's revelations had on the international community. This chapter delves into the multifaceted dimensions of this global landscape, exploring the diverse responses and initiatives that emerged as countries contended with the far-reaching implications of mass surveillance in the digital age.

Immediate Responses from World Governments

In the aftermath of Edward Snowden's unprecedented leak of classified information on global surveillance programs, world governments were jolted into action. The revelations sparked a flurry of responses from nations across the globe, each struggling to come to terms with the scope and implications of the disclosed activities. The immediacy of these responses underscored the gravity of Snowden's disclosures and the widespread impact they had on international relations and governance.

Governments swiftly initiated high-level discussions and emergency meetings to assess the potential ramifications of the leaked information. This led to a complex web of reactions, varying from public condemnation to behind-the-scenes diplomatic maneuvering. Some countries openly expressed outrage at the intrusive nature of the surveillance tactics revealed, viewing them as a breach of sovereignty and individual rights. Others, while publicly denouncing the actions, privately grappled with their own involvement or complicity in similar surveillance programs.

Within this context, a spectrum of responses emerged, shaped by geopolitical considerations, alliances, and domestic political pressures. The shockwaves reverberated through traditional allies and adversaries alike, prompting reassessments of trust and cooperation. Complicating matters further, the potential impact on intelligence-sharing agreements and security collaborations loomed large, raising critical questions about mutual trust and transparency among nations.

As the global community navigated this uncharted territory, divergent views surfaced on the appropriate course of action. Calls for accountability and systemic reforms gained traction, challenging the status quo and demanding greater transparency in government operations. Simultaneously, some governments intensified their efforts to enhance cybersecurity measures and counter foreign espionage, heightening the sense of urgency in safeguarding national interests.

The immediate responses from world governments to Snowden's disclosures set the stage for a prolonged period of introspection and recalibration in international affairs. The inherent tension between security imperatives and individual freedoms crystallized in the wake of these revelations, spawning a broader discourse on the delicate balance between surveillance capabilities and civil liberties. This chapter marks a critical juncture in the book, shedding light on the multilayered repercussions and strategic considerations that underscored the international response to Snowden's disclosures.

International Law and Privacy Rights

The revelations brought forth by Edward Snowden reverberated across the globe, touching on core issues of international law and privacy rights. The exposure of widespread surveillance activities raised critical questions about the legality of such practices under international law. With the rights to privacy enshrined in numerous international treaties and conventions, the disclosures sparked a heated debate regarding the compliance of government surveillance programs with these legal frameworks. In response to Snowden's disclosures, legal experts, human rights advocates, and policymakers engaged in robust discussions about the implications of mass surveillance on the fundamental rights of individuals and the broader implications for international law. The tension between national security concerns and individual privacy rights underscored the need to reexamine established legal norms in light of technological advancements and evolving security threats. As governments grappled with the fallout of the disclosures, the concept of privacy in an interconnected world took center stage in ongoing legal debates. The unprecedented scope of surveillance activities revealed by Snowden prompted calls for the reevaluation and reinforcement of existing legal protections for privacy at the international level. Concerns over extraterritorial reach and the potential infringements on the privacy rights of individuals outside a country's borders added layers of complexity to the legal discourse surrounding surveillance practices. Moreover, the interplay between national sovereignty and transnational data flows highlighted the intricate balance required to safeguard privacy rights in a globally connected digital landscape. At the heart of these deliberations lay the foundational principles of human rights law, which demanded careful examination and reinterpretation in the context of contemporary surveillance capabilities. The evolving landscape of technology and its impact on privacy rights necessitated a comprehensive review of international legal instruments to ensure their adequacy in addressing the challenges posed by modern surveillance. The nuanced interconnections between privacy, security, and the rule of law underscored the imperative for cohesive, rights-respecting responses within the framework of international law. The legacy of Snowden's disclosures continues to influence ongoing efforts to strengthen the protection of privacy rights within the global legal landscape.

Diplomatic Strains and Allegations

The revelations brought forth by Edward Snowden's disclosures had far-reaching consequences that extended beyond domestic borders. As governments grappled with the magnitude of the leaked information, diplomatic relations between various countries strained under the weight of allegations and suspicions. The United States, in particular, faced mounting pressure from its allies and adversaries alike, as they sought explanations for the extent of the surveillance activities as detailed in the leaks.

Allegations of espionage and breach of trust emerged as diplomatic conversations turned tense. Traditional allies of the United States expressed outrage and concern over the implications of the disclosed surveillance programs. Relations between the U.S. and countries such as Germany, France, and Brazil, among others, were significantly strained, with leaders calling for transparency and accountability. The severity of the strain was evident in the unprecedented summoning of U.S. ambassadors and officials to address the allegations, disrupting established diplomatic norms.

At the same time, accusations of complicity and collaboration in surveillance activities also arose among allies in international intelligence-sharing agreements. The interconnected nature of global surveillance networks led to a web of allegations and counter-allegations as nations sought to distance themselves from any involvement in the controversial practices revealed by Snowden's leaks.

The diplomatic strains resulting from the Snowden disclosures precipitated a reevaluation of trust and cooperation among nations and alliances. These events underscored the profound impact of surveillance activities on international diplomacy and exposed the fragility of global relationships amid allegations of misconduct. Furthermore, the aftermath of these strained relations reverberated in subsequent discussions on cybersecurity, data privacy, and the need for clear protocols regarding international intelligence operations.

The complexities of diplomatic strains and allegations following the Snowden revelations serve as a critical aspect of understanding the broader implications of mass surveillance on global affairs. This period marked a pivotal juncture in international relations, sparking debates on sovereignty, security, and the balance of power that continue to resonate in contemporary political discourse."

Tech Industry Reaction and Reform

The revelations brought forth by Edward Snowden's disclosures ignited a seismic shift within the global tech industry. Companies confronted an existential dilemma as they grappled with the knowledge that their products and services had been co-opted by government surveillance programs. The widespread public outcry catalyzed intense soul-searching and introspection across the technology sector. Leaders in the industry, accustomed to innovating at breakneck speeds, now found themselves at a crossroads, forced to confront complex ethical and legal considerations. At the heart of this seismic reevaluation lay a fundamental question: What responsibilities did these tech giants have in safeguarding the privacy and civil liberties of their users? In response to the pervasive sense of betrayal and breach of trust, several prominent tech companies took bold and unprecedented steps to fortify their commitment to user privacy and data security. Encryption became a focal point as companies sought to shore up their defenses against unwarranted intrusion. Stronger measures were implemented to resist government requests for user data, signaling a resolute determination to protect customer information from clandestine surveillance. Simultaneously, the revelations served as a catalyst for introspection and collective advocacy within the tech community. Industry leaders galvanized efforts to advocate for legislative reform, emphasizing the need for more transparent and judicious surveillance policies. Moreover, a wave of transparency reports emerged, shedding light on government requests for user data and striving to mitigate the opacity that had shrouded such practices in secrecy. As the wave of reform gained momentum, companies strove to bolster their commitment to user rights and privacy. They endeavored to redefine their role as stewards of digital integrity, demonstrating a newfound allegiance to the principles that underpin a free and open internet. This transformative period saw a remarkable convergence of technological innovation and ethical imperative, propelling the tech industry into uncharted territory. Yet, even as companies mounted their defenses in the name of user privacy, they encountered formidable obstacles, navigating through a labyrinth of legal constraints and national security directives. The journey toward reform was fraught with complexities, underscoring the intricate interplay between corporate responsibility, national security imperatives, and individual freedoms. The landscape of the tech industry was irrevocably altered, forever bearing the indelible imprint of a watershed moment that compelled an industry-wide reexamination of its values and obligations.

UN Involvement and Global Discussions

The revelations brought forward by Edward Snowden's disclosures concerning mass surveillance sparked intense global discussions and prompted involvement from various international entities, including the United Nations. As the public and policymakers around the world grappled with the implications of widespread government surveillance programs, the UN became a focal point for fostering dialogue and deliberation on these critical matters. UN involvement in the aftermath of the Snowden leaks can be observed through several key initiatives and forums.

One of the prominent responses from the United Nations was the consideration of privacy as a fundamental human right in the digital age. This led to the establishment of the Special Rapporteur on the Right to Privacy, who played a pivotal role in addressing the challenges posed by mass surveillance and the protection of privacy rights on a global scale. The rapporteur's reports and recommendations served as a foundation for shaping the discourse on privacy and surveillance within the UN and its member states.

Furthermore, the UN General Assembly became a platform for impassioned debates and resolutions related to governmental surveillance practices and their impact on individual privacy rights. Member states engaged in comprehensive discussions regarding the ethical and legal boundaries of surveillance, emphasizing the need to strike a balance between national security concerns and the protection of civil liberties. The gravity of the issue led to the adoption of landmark resolutions calling for a thorough review of surveillance policies with respect to international law and human rights standards.

In addition to formal sessions, the UN hosted expert panels and symposiums dedicated to examining the intersection of technology, privacy, and state surveillance. These gatherings convened renowned technologists, legal scholars, and human rights advocates to explore viable strategies for advancing accountable and transparent surveillance practices. The exchange of diverse viewpoints and expertise has been instrumental in shaping nuanced perspectives on the complexities of surveillance governance and bolstering global efforts towards fostering a rights-based approach to digital monitoring.

Moreover, the UN's engagement extended to collaborating with regional organizations and civil society groups to address cross-border implications of mass surveillance. Through collaborative dialogues and joint research initiatives, the UN sought to amplify the voices of affected individuals and communities, while also devising mechanisms for safeguarding human rights in an interconnected world marked by extensive data collection and analysis.

Overall, the UN's involvement and facilitation of global conversations following the Snowden disclosures have significantly redefined the narrative surrounding surveillance, privacy rights, and democratic principles. By leveraging its platforms and networks, the United Nations has galvanized a collective, multidimensional response to the challenges posed by mass surveillance, thereby reinforcing the imperative to uphold individual freedoms and dignity in the digital era.

Surveillance Policy Reevaluation Worldwide

In the wake of Edward Snowden's revelations, governments around the world have been compelled to critically reevaluate their surveillance policies. The exposure of extensive and intrusive surveillance programs sparked widespread concerns about the balance between national security and individual privacy rights. As a result, countries from diverse regions have embarked on comprehensive reviews of their surveillance laws and practices with the aim of addressing public apprehension and ensuring accountability. This global wave of introspection is characterized by distinct trends and responses that reflect the complex interplay of legal, ethical, and technological considerations.

In many democratic nations, including the United States, the United Kingdom, and Germany, the disclosures prompted intense debates within legislative bodies, leading to the introduction of reform proposals aimed at enhancing oversight and transparency of surveillance activities. Key provisions under scrutiny include the authorization procedures for data collection, the scope of permissible targets, and the mechanisms for judicial review of surveillance operations. Moreover, there has been a growing emphasis on strengthening protections for human rights and civil liberties in the context of intelligence gathering.

Conversely, authoritarian regimes and non-democratic states have faced heightened scrutiny and condemnation from the international community for their expansive surveillance apparatuses, often employed as tools of repression and control. The revelations have catalyzed discussions on the implications for international relations and human rights standards, prompting calls for greater accountability and adherence to universal norms. This has necessitated concerted efforts by international organizations and diplomatic channels to address the cross-border implications of pervasive surveillance practices.

Furthermore, the globalization of digital communication networks has underscored the need for coordinated international frameworks governing data protection and privacy. The European Union's enactment of the General Data Protection Regulation (GDPR) stands as a prominent example of a legislative response aimed at harmonizing data privacy laws and safeguarding personal information in the digital age. This shift towards more rigorous data protection standards has reverberated across continents, influencing the formulation of new guidelines and regulations in pursuit of an interconnected framework for the governance of surveillance and data collection.

The reevaluation of surveillance policies at a global scale has engendered a rich tapestry of legal and policy developments, reflecting the enduring impact of Edward Snowden's disclosures on the contemporary landscape of intelligence and privacy. While disparate in their specific approaches, these initiatives collectively signify a fundamental reexamination of the societal contract surrounding surveillance, emphasizing the imperative of upholding fundamental rights in the face of evolving technological capabilities and security imperatives.

Public Protests and Civic Activism

The disclosure of extensive surveillance practices unleashed a wave of public protests and civic activism on a global scale. Citizens, advocacy groups, and civil society organizations mobilized to express their concerns about privacy violations and governmental overreach. In numerous countries, individuals took to the streets with placards and slogans, passionately demanding accountability and transparency from their governments. These demonstrations served as a powerful testament to the collective desire for safeguarding fundamental rights in the face of unchecked surveillance activities.

Citizens participating in these protests were driven by a deeply-rooted commitment to upholding democratic values and principles. They voiced their dissent against intrusive surveillance measures that encroached upon personal privacy and freedom of expression. Civil liberties advocates and human rights organizations played pivotal roles in orchestrating these movements, utilizing social media platforms and grassroots campaigns to amplify their message and garner widespread support.

Simultaneously, civic activism flourished through petitions, legal challenges, and community events aimed at fostering public dialogue surrounding the implications of mass surveillance. The emergence of grassroots initiatives and digital activism further underscored the diversified strategies employed by concerned citizens to engage with the complex issue of government surveillance.

The impact of public protests and civic activism reverberated beyond national borders. It inspired transnational solidarity movements and galvanized collaborative efforts among advocacy networks to address the global dimensions of privacy infringement and information security. By shedding light on pervasive state surveillance practices, these movements fueled a shared resolve to defend individual autonomy and preserve the integrity of democratic societies.

In response to the heightened public awareness and mobilization, governments faced mounting pressure to recalibrate their surveillance policies and enact safeguards to protect citizens' rights. This chapter seeks to illuminate the indelible imprint of public protests and civic activism as catalysts for instigating profound societal introspection and spurring legislative reforms in the sphere of surveillance and data privacy.

Data Protection Initiatives in the EU and Beyond

In the wake of the revelations brought to light by Edward Snowden, the issue of data protection gained renewed urgency on a global scale, particularly within the European Union (EU). As a fundamental right, the protection of personal data is enshrined in the EU's legal framework, further amplified by the General Data Protection Regulation (GDPR) that came into effect in 2018. This landmark legislation not only enhanced the rights of individuals regarding their personal data but also imposed stringent obligations on organizations handling such data, irrespective of their location. The Snowden disclosures acted as a catalyst, prompting policymakers and regulators in the EU to fortify data protection laws and mechanisms. Beyond the EU, similar initiatives emerged in other jurisdictions where concerns regarding mass surveillance and data privacy violations were heightened. Countries reassessed their existing laws to align with evolving technological advancements and address the potential abuse of surveillance capabilities.

In the United States, for example, debates around privacy and security intensified, leading to proposed reforms and public discourse concerning the balance between national security imperatives and civil liberties. Moreover, collaboration between nations on data protection gained momentum, fostering discussions around international standards and norms pertaining to digital privacy. The landmark Schrems II ruling by the Court of Justice of the European Union further underscored the significance of protecting personal data, especially when transferred across borders. This ruling had profound implications for international data transfers, provoking a reevaluation of data protection measures and safeguards beyond the EU's borders. The prominence of privacy-focused technology and the rise of encrypted communications tools marked a shift in the digital landscape, reflecting growing consumer demands for privacy-preserving solutions. Companies and developers responded by incorporating privacy-enhancing features into their products, indicating a paradigm shift toward proactive data protection measures. Furthermore, civil society organizations and advocacy groups played a pivotal role in advocating for robust data protection frameworks globally, amplifying the imperative of safeguarding individuals' privacy rights in an increasingly interconnected world. This confluence of regulatory developments, technological innovations, and societal awareness highlights the enduring impact of Edward Snowden's disclosures on reshaping the discourse and implementation of data protection initiatives in the EU and beyond.

Summary

In summary, the global response to the revelations brought forth by Edward Snowden's disclosures has been nothing short of transformative. Across the European Union and in other regions worldwide, legislative and regulatory actions have been enacted to reinforce data protection measures in an effort to safeguard the privacy rights of citizens amid mounting concerns over surveillance practices. The implications of these initiatives have reverberated not only within domestic jurisdictions but also in international legal and diplomatic arenas, prompting a shift in how governments approach intelligence-gathering activities and cross-border data flows. As we move forward, the focus will turn to analyzing the long-term effects of these regulatory changes and their impact on global cyber policies and international relations.

8

The Snowden Files and Media Frenzy

The Media Explosion

The media explosion that followed Edward Snowden's disclosures was unprecedented in its scale and impact. As soon as the initial revelations surfaced, a whirlwind of global media attention engulfed the story, propelling it into the forefront of public consciousness. News outlets around the world scrambled to cover the shocking revelations, and the scope of the coverage was immense. Traditional print and broadcast media, as well as online news platforms, all devoted extensive resources to analyzing and disseminating the leaked information. From the United States to Europe, Asia, and beyond, the reach of the coverage was truly global, reflecting the universal significance of the issues at hand. The explosive nature of the leaks ensured that the story captured the attention not only of governments and policymakers but also of ordinary citizens who were eager to comprehend the far-reaching implications of Snowden's disclosures. This intense and widespread scrutiny set the stage for a profound reshaping of public discourse around surveillance, privacy, and government transparency.

Initial Disclosures: The Role of The Guardian and Washington Post

In the wake of Edward Snowden's unprecedented leak, two renowned news outlets, The Guardian and The Washington Post, played pivotal roles in disseminating the classified information to the public. Their involvement marked a watershed moment in the history of investigative journalism, raising crucial ethical and legal questions while sparking intense global debate. The initial disclosures by these publications not only brought to light the extent of government surveillance but also initiated a profound reevaluation of privacy rights and national security measures. The Guardian, a British publication, was the first to break the story on June 5, 2013. It unveiled the top-secret documents provided by Snowden, revealing the magnitude of the National Security Agency's (NSA) surveillance programs, including the collection of metadata from millions of Americans' communications. This bombshell report, authored by journalist Glenn Greenwald, sent shockwaves throughout the world and triggered a flurry of reactions from both the public and government entities. In parallel, The Washington Post, another venerable institution, released its own articles based on the trove of classified materials obtained from Snowden. The Post's coverage delved into the intricacies of the NSA's surveillance operations, providing detailed insights into the agency's widespread data collection practices and their implications for individual privacy. The reporting by both newspapers facilitated an open dialogue about the balance between national security and civil liberties, forcing citizens and policymakers to grapple with the implications of unchecked government surveillance. Additionally, the collaboration between The Guardian and The Washington Post exemplified the power of the press to hold governmental institutions accountable, demonstrating the critical role that investigative journalism plays in a democratic society. As the revelations continued to unfold, the journalistic responsibility and duty to accurately inform the public were put to the test, leading to contentious discussions around the ethics of publishing classified information.

Nevertheless, the initial disclosures by these reputable publications set the stage for a series of events that would forever alter the global discourse on surveillance, transparency, and individual privacy.

Snowden's Strategic Media Engagement

Edward Snowden's actions were not limited to the release of classified materials; they also involved meticulous strategic planning for their dissemination. Recognizing the power of media in shaping public discourse, Snowden strategically engaged with various journalists and media outlets to ensure that the information reached a global audience. His approach encompassed several key elements that distinguished his engagement from typical leaks. Firstly, Snowden was intentional about partnering with reputable journalists like Glenn Greenwald and Laura Poitras, who possessed the expertise and ethical standards necessary for handling the sensitive material. This deliberate choice aimed to lend credibility and gravity to the disclosures, ensuring that they would be taken seriously by the public and policymakers alike. Additionally, Snowden's orchestrated release of information aimed to maximize impact without compromising security. He maintained a careful balance, gradually revealing details to sustain public attention while safeguarding operational intelligence. Snowden's calculated timing and controlled delivery of revelations heightened their influence and sustained media coverage, catalyzing intense public debate on surveillance practices and privacy rights. Furthermore, Snowden utilized channels beyond traditional print and broadcast media, leveraging the reach and immediacy of digital platforms. Through encrypted communication and online forums, he extended the conversation directly to a diverse online audience, circumventing conventional constraints and broadening the scope of the dialogue. This adept use of modern technology paralleled the digital nature of the disclosed surveillance programs, aligning with Snowden's broader aims of sparking a comprehensive reevaluation of contemporary surveillance practices. As the media frenzy around the disclosures intensified, Snowden deftly navigated the spotlight, maintaining a strategic presence to articulate the underlying rationale for his actions. By engaging with the media not as a reactionary figure but as an informed advocate, Snowden was able to shape the narrative surrounding the leaks, emphasizing their societal significance and ethical implications. In doing so, he catalyzed profound introspection on the interplay between national security imperatives, individual privacy, and government accountability. Snowden's acute awareness of the media landscape and his adroit navigation of it greatly amplified the impact of his revelations, catalyzing a seismic shift in public consciousness and policy discourse.

Key Documents and Their Revelations

The key documents brought to light by Edward Snowden form the backbone of the revelations that shook the world. These classified documents encompassed a diverse array of programs and activities conducted by government intelligence agencies, shedding unprecedented light on the global surveillance apparatus. Among the most significant disclosures were revelations regarding mass data collection programs such as PRISM and the bulk collection of telecommunications metadata. Furthermore, the leaked documents exposed the extensive cooperation between government authorities and major technology companies, unveiling the intricate workings of surveillance partnerships.

The significance of these revelations cannot be overstated, as they provided irrefutable evidence of the far-reaching scope of surveillance activities, both domestically and internationally. In doing so, these disclosures sparked widespread and urgent debates on privacy rights, government accountability, and the balance of power between national security imperatives and individual freedoms. Moreover, the documents revealed the extent to which citizens' personal communications and digital footprints were subject to systematic monitoring, raising profound ethical and legal questions that resonated globally.

By delving into the specifics of each document and their implications, this chapter will unravel the intricate details of the surveillance programs and their impact on civil liberties. It will explore how these revelations fundamentally altered public perceptions of government surveillance and prompted a reassessment of established norms and practices. Additionally, the chapter will provide insights into the reactions of various stakeholders, including policymakers, technology corporations, and advocacy groups, in response to the unprecedented disclosures.

Ultimately, the examination of key documents and their revelations is essential in comprehending the magnitude of Snowden's disclosures and their enduring effects on the realms of politics, law, and technology. By meticulously dissecting the content of these documents and illuminating their ramifications, this chapter seeks to provide a comprehensive understanding of the profound impact of the disclosures on contemporary society.

Journalistic Ethics and Responsibilities

In the midst of the media frenzy surrounding the Snowden files, a critical examination of journalistic ethics and responsibilities comes to the forefront. The ethical considerations that journalists face when reporting on sensitive classified information are manifold. They must carefully weigh the public's right to know against potential harm to national security and individuals involved. Journalists have a responsibility to verify the authenticity of the leaked documents and ensure their reporting is accurate, fair, and balanced. Additionally, they must consider the broader societal implications of their reporting, including the potential impact on diplomatic relations and global security. This ethical dilemma raises profound questions about the role of the press in a democratic society.

Moreover, the responsibility of journalists extends to protecting their sources, especially in cases involving whistleblowers like Edward Snowden. The ethical practice of not revealing the identity of sources is crucial to maintaining trust and encouraging others to come forward with important information in the future. However, this commitment can also lead to legal and professional challenges for journalists who may face pressure from authorities to disclose their sources. Balancing the need for transparency and accountability with the protection of sources is a complex ethical tightrope that journalists must navigate.

Furthermore, as the Snowden revelations sparked intense public debate and controversy, journalists were challenged to provide comprehensive and nuanced coverage while avoiding sensationalism. Responsible reporting required careful contextualization of the leaked information, presenting it in a manner that promoted understanding without unduly magnifying fear or alarm. Ethical journalism demands a commitment to truth-seeking and a dedication to providing the public with well-informed, thoughtful analysis.

The ethical obligations of journalists in the wake of the Snowden files underscore the profound impact of their work on shaping public discourse and influencing policy decisions. By examining the choices made by journalists in disseminating the information disclosed by Snowden, we gain insight into the complexities of media ethics and the weighty responsibilities that accompany the power of the press. This chapter delves deeply into the intricate realm of journalistic ethics and responsibilities, shedding light on the pivotal role that journalists play in informing and shaping our understanding of significant events.

Public Reaction: Outrage, Support, and Debate

The release of the Snowden files triggered a complex tapestry of public reaction, characterized by a tripartite blend of outrage, support, and debate. As the revelations within the leaked documents began to unfold in the public sphere, they ignited a firestorm of emotion and discourse that reverberated across the global populace. Outrage permeated through individuals who were shocked and appalled by the scale and reach of the surveillance programs. The blatant intrusion into personal privacy and the erosion of civil liberties struck a chord with many, leading to a groundswell of indignation and protest. As the shockwaves of outrage surged, they collided with an undercurrent of unsparing support for Edward Snowden's audacious act of whistleblowing. A faction emerged steadfastly championing Snowden as an emblem of courage and moral conviction. This wave of support transcended geographical borders, uniting individuals who applauded Snowden's resolve to expose the clandestine practices carried out in the name of national security. Across digital platforms and street demonstrations, expressions of solidarity proliferated, forming a counterbalance to the prevailing outrage.In the midst of this tumultuous collision between outrage and support, a broader societal debate blossomed, punctuated by diverging viewpoints and deliberative exchanges. Legal experts, policymakers, and everyday citizens engaged in a discourse that traversed ethical, legal, and societal considerations. Conversations stemming from the leaked files transcended the specifics of individual revelations, delving into the broader ramifications of pervasive surveillance in the digital age. The debate encompassed discussions on the delicate equilibrium between security and privacy, the oversight of intelligence agencies, and the implications for democratic societies.Group dynamics played out on social media platforms, with conversations rapidly evolving into multifaceted dialogues, knitting together disparate perspectives. Counterarguments, endorsements, and calls for action melded into a symphony of civic engagement, ultimately solidifying the Snowden disclosures as a catalyst for profound introspection and dialogic evolution. Public reaction, spanning the spectrum from heated indignation to unwavering advocacy, served as a testament to the seismic impact of the Snowden files on the global consciousness. This chapter serves as a granular exploration of the multifaceted response elicited by the disclosures, capturing the intricacies of human sentiment as it intersected with the unprecedented revelations unveiled by Edward Snowden.

Governmental Responses to Media Coverage

The media frenzy ignited by Edward Snowden's disclosures sent shockwaves through governments worldwide, prompting an array of responses that vividly underscored the gravity and sensitivity of the leaked information. As the revelations reverberated across international news outlets, governments swiftly moved to address and contain the repercussions of these confidential disclosures.

In response to media coverage, governments around the world scrambled to assess the extent of the disclosed information and the potential impact on national security. The initial reactions ranged from vehement denials and discrediting of Snowden's motives to outright condemnation of the leaks as a betrayal of state secrets. In the United States, government officials vehemently condemned the media coverage of Snowden's revelations, with some labeling him as a traitor and demanding his immediate extradition for prosecution. Conversely, other nations displayed a more reserved approach, acknowledging the serious nature of the leaks while refraining from overtly antagonizing the exposer or plunging into confrontational rhetoric.

Furthermore, governmental responses to media coverage also entailed strategic damage control and narrative shaping. In an effort to mitigate the fallout from the media storm, government agencies sought to downplay the significance of the disclosed information, emphasizing the necessity of clandestine surveillance programs for national security interests and framing the disclosures as detrimental to public safety. Concurrently, efforts were directed towards discrediting Snowden himself, portraying him as an unreliable source and casting doubt on the authenticity of the leaked documents. This calculated narrative management aimed to sway public opinion and attenuate the resonance of Snowden's disclosures.

Additionally, the governmental responses to media coverage illuminated the intricate interplay between press freedom, state secrecy, and the public's right to know. The tensions between these fundamental pillars of democracy surfaced prominently amidst the media maelstrom, with governments wrestling to reconcile the imperative of transparent governance with the imperatives of national security, all while grappling with the ramifications of mass exposure of classified intelligence gathering activities. These responses unfolded against a backdrop of intense debates on the limits of governmental authority in surveilling its citizens and the ethical quandaries inherent in balancing privacy rights with security imperatives.

Ultimately, the diverse manifestations of governmental responses to media coverage reflected the far-reaching repercussions of Snowden's courageous act, stirring profound introspection within political echelons and prompting a reevaluation of the ethical and legal frameworks governing intelligence operations. The clashes between governmental authorities and the free press burgeoned into a pivotal juncture in modern history, signifying a watershed moment in the evolving dynamics between state power, media scrutiny, and individual liberties.

Impact on Global News Networks

The disclosure of the Snowden files triggered a seismic shift in global news networks, reshaping the way news was reported and consumed. The revelations unleashed by Edward Snowden were a wakeup call to journalistic institutions worldwide, signaling the dawn of a new era in investigative reporting. Each major news outlet faced a critical decision —how to handle the deluge of classified information that threatened to redefine the landscape of public discourse. Some embraced the opportunity to break groundbreaking stories, while others approached the delicate matter with caution, mindful of the ethical implications and potential backlash.

The impact stretched far beyond the traditional boundaries of journalism. With the proliferation of digital media platforms, the dissemination of these revelations reverberated across continents at an unprecedented pace. News organizations swiftly adapted their strategies to accommodate this rapidly shifting paradigm, leveraging technological advancements to transcend geographical limitations and engage a global audience. In doing so, they heralded a new age of transparency and accountability, compelling governments and corporations to confront uncomfortable truths and demanding greater scrutiny from the public.

Notably, the Snowden files compelled global news networks to reassess their relationships with governmental entities. Long-established dynamics were challenged as media institutions navigated the complex terrain between watchdog journalism and national security concerns. The inherent tension between the rights of the press and the imperatives of statecraft came to the fore, prompting introspection and debate within newsrooms worldwide. This period marked a renaissance of investigative journalism, fostering a climate where courageous reporters braved formidable obstacles to uphold the principles of a free press.

Furthermore, the impact on global news networks transcended the immediate furore surrounding the disclosures. It sparked a broader conversation about the responsibilities of news organizations in a world redefined by ubiquitous surveillance. Ethical considerations took center stage, guiding conscientious journalists through the moral labyrinth of reporting on sensitive intelligence operations. The enduring legacy of the Snowden revelations lies in the indelible imprint it left on the ethos of investigative journalism, igniting a sustained commitment to holding power to account and safeguarding democratic principles.

In sum, the impact of the Snowden files on global news networks was transformative, precipitating a renaissance of investigative journalism and stimulating a widespread dialogue on the nexus of press freedom, national security, and the public interest. As the reverberations continue to shape contemporary discourse, the enduring ramifications underscore the profound influence of whistleblowers in catalyzing societal change and galvanizing the media to serve as an unwavering sentinel of truth and integrity.

The Role of Social Media in Amplifying the Message

Social media platforms played a pivotal role in amplifying Edward Snowden's message and disclosures to a global audience. As the news broke, individuals across the world took to platforms such as Twitter, Facebook, and Reddit to share, discuss, and debate the revelations brought forth by Snowden and the media outlets reporting on his leaks. This widespread dissemination of information through social media had an unprecedented effect on both the dissemination and reception of the leaked documents.

One significant aspect of social media's impact was its ability to rapidly and widely propagate information. Stories and updates related to Snowden trended across various platforms, ensuring that the public remained engaged with the evolving narrative. The instantaneous nature of social media allowed for real-time discussions and analyses, enabling the general populace to participate in shaping the discourse surrounding surveillance, privacy, and government accountability.

Moreover, social media provided a platform for dissenting voices to challenge traditional narratives presented by mainstream media. It fostered an environment where diverse perspectives and interpretations could coexist, driving nuanced conversations about the implications of the leaked information. This multifaceted dialogue contributed to a more comprehensive understanding of the issues at hand and encouraged critical thinking among audiences worldwide.

Furthermore, the democratizing effect of social media empowered individuals to become active participants in the whistleblowing saga. Through the use of hashtags, direct messaging, and viral content sharing, people were able to express solidarity with Snowden, mobilize support for his cause, and coordinate grassroots activism. This collective digital movement not only influenced public opinion but also exerted pressure on policymakers and institutions, demanding transparency and accountability regarding surveillance practices.

However, it is essential to acknowledge the challenges posed by social media in this context. The sheer volume of information shared online often led to misinformation and sensationalism, potentially diluting the core messages of Snowden's disclosures. Additionally, the intense polarization of opinions within these digital spaces sometimes hindered constructive dialogue, perpetuating echo chambers and reinforcing existing biases.

In conclusion, the role of social media in amplifying Edward Snowden's message transcended mere exposure; it catalyzed a global conversation, reshaped public discourse, and mobilized a diverse array of voices. By leveraging the far-reaching influence of social media, Snowden's revelations permeated through societies, sparking crucial debates on privacy, security, and governmental transparency.

Summary and Transition to Legal Challenges

The converging forces of traditional media, combined with the pervasive influence of social media, helped propel Edward Snowden's revelations into the global spotlight. These disclosures sparked a sea of reactions from individuals, governments, and organizations, giving rise to significant ethical, legal, and diplomatic dilemmas. As the media frenzy unfolded, the interplay between journalism, freedom of speech, and national security became a focal point for public discourse.

The summary of this period encapsulates a watershed moment in contemporary history, marked by the immense power of information dissemination. It underscores the intricate dynamics between whistle-blowing, investigative journalism, and the emergence of the digital age. Analyzing the impact of social media on amplifying Snowden's message provides unique insights into how information transcends borders and engages diverse audiences on a global scale.

Transitioning from the media frenzy, the narrative shifts to the impending legal challenges that snowballed in the wake of the disclosures. As governments grappled with the far-reaching implications of the leaked information, legal battles ensued, shaping the trajectory of Snowden's ongoing saga. Detailing the multifaceted legal challenges and controversies encountered by Snowden illuminates the complex interplay between individual rights, government authority, and international law. The ensuing chapters delve into the intricate web of legal entanglements, framing them within the broader context of civil liberties, state surveillance, and the pursuit of justice.

The transition to legal challenges serves as a crucial pivot point for navigating the intricate aftermath of Snowden's actions. By examining the legal landscape both domestically and internationally, this section unearths the riveting complexities that lay at the intersection of law, politics, and morality. It sets the stage for an in-depth exploration of the enduring legal battles and diplomatic tensions that continue to shape the legacy of Edward Snowden, offering a compelling insight into the relentless struggle for transparency and accountability within contemporary governance.

9

Legal Entanglements: Charges and Diplomatic Tensions

Legal Charges

The legal charges brought against Edward Snowden are primarily grounded in the context of the Espionage Act, a statute introduced during World War I to combat espionage and unauthorized disclosure of sensitive information that could potentially harm the United States or benefit its adversaries. The Act has been heavily scrutinized for its broad scope and severe penalties, as it applies not only to spies and traitors but also journalists, whistleblowers, and anyone disclosing national defense information without proper authorization. Edward Snowden's disclosures, which exposed widespread government surveillance programs, have led to his indictment under the Espionage Act. The initial accusations focused on Snowden's alleged unauthorized communication and dissemination of classified information to the media, particularly regarding the National Security Agency's surveillance activities. Such revelations were deemed by the U.S. government as potentially detrimental to national security interests and were met with swift legal action. While Snowden has argued that his actions were driven by a civic duty to expose unconstitutional and invasive surveillance practices, the legal framework under the Espionage Act holds him accountable for disclosing classified intelligence. This collision of perspectives has resulted in a complex legal battle with far-reaching implications.

The Espionage Act: Historical Context and Application

Enacted during World War I in 1917, the Espionage Act is a pivotal piece of legislation that has echoed through the corridors of power and justice for over a century. Designed with the primary intent of addressing espionage and curbing the dissemination of information that could compromise national security, this act provided the federal government with unprecedented powers to prosecute individuals engaged in activities deemed detrimental to the United States' interests. Its historical context is deeply intertwined with the turbulent sociopolitical landscape of the early 20th century, shaped by the specter of war, fervent nationalism, and a climate of fear. The Espionage Act's passage reflected the government's ardent efforts to maintain control and prevent any perceived obstruction of its war endeavors.

Since its inception, the application of the Espionage Act has extended beyond conventional wartime scenarios to encompass various definitions of national security threats, resulting in a complex web of legal precedents and contentious interpretations. The case law surrounding the Espionage Act has been marked by recurring debates on the delicate balance between safeguarding classified information and respecting the constitutional rights of free speech and press. This ongoing discourse has underscored the inherent tension between governmental authority and individual liberties, especially in the digital era where information flows across borders at unprecedented speed and volume, challenging traditional notions of security and secrecy.

Edward Snowden's disclosure of classified documents in 2013 reignited the relevance and scrutiny of the Espionage Act, thrusting it into the center of a global conversation about surveillance, transparency, and accountability. The charged environment surrounding Snowden's actions placed the Espionage Act under intense public and legal scrutiny, exposing its potential ramifications for whistleblowers and journalists alike. This pivotal juncture underscored the enduring significance of this century-old statute within the contemporary landscape of national security, freedom of information, and the evolving role of technology in the exercise of power and oversight. As we delve deeper into the intricacies of the Espionage Act and its implications, we unravel a narrative woven from the threads of history, statecraft, and the relentless pursuit of truth and justice.

Following Edward Snowden's disclosure of classified information in 2013, the U.S. government's response was swift and resolute. The revelations pertaining to mass surveillance programs conducted by the National Security Agency (NSA) and other intelligence agencies stirred a maelstrom of political, legal, and diplomatic ramifications. In response to these disclosures, the U.S. government embarked on an aggressive pursuit of Snowden and levied multiple charges against him, including violations of the Espionage Act.

The government's reaction demonstrated its unwavering commitment to safeguarding national security and preserving the integrity of its intelligence operations. This sparked a contentious debate within the public sphere and among policymakers, with opinions sharply divided on whether Snowden's actions constituted whistleblowing or treason. Moreover, the government's stance on the matter underscored the severity of the situation, portraying Snowden as a threat to the nation's security posture.

As initial charges were announced, the breadth and depth of the government's legal response became palpable. The U.S. Department of Justice pursued charges of theft of government property and unauthorized communication of national defense information against Snowden, carrying severe penalties. Grand jury indictments preserved the gravity of these accusations, setting the stage for a protracted legal battle between the U.S. government and Snowden.

The impact of these charges reverberated in both domestic and international arenas, amplifying the complexities inherent in Snowden's revelation. Internationally, the U.S. government's reaction strained diplomatic relations with several nations as Snowden sought asylum abroad. The charges escalated tensions and raised profound questions regarding the delicate balance between national security imperatives and individual liberties.

In summary, the U.S. government's reaction and initial charges against Edward Snowden constituted a pivotal juncture in the unfolding narrative of his whistleblowing saga. These events precipitated a series of legal entanglements and evoked fervent discussions about the boundaries of state authority, the rights of whistleblowers, and the ramifications of mass surveillance. The repercussions of the U.S. government's reaction and initial charges continue to reverberate, shaping the contours of the ongoing discourse surrounding privacy, security, and individual freedom in the digital age.

International Law Considerations

The legal implications of Edward Snowden's whistleblowing extend beyond domestic jurisdictions and raise complex issues related to international law. As Snowden's actions reverberated across the global landscape, a web of legal considerations emerged, prompting scrutiny regarding the interactions between national sovereignty and transnational obligations.

One overarching concern pertains to the extraterritorial reach of U.S. surveillance activities disclosed by Snowden. This has sparked debates surrounding the extent to which the United States' intelligence operations infringe upon the sovereign rights of other nations. International legal scholars have debated the compatibility of these actions with established principles such as territorial integrity, non-interference, and respect for the legal systems of other states.

Furthermore, questions have arisen regarding the impact of Snowden's revelations on international human rights law. The mass surveillance programs unveiled by Snowden raised concerns about the right to privacy and protection against arbitrary interference enshrined in international human rights instruments. This prompted critical assessments of the balance between national security imperatives and individual freedoms, warranting discussions on the evolving contours of privacy rights in the digital age.

Another contentious area of analysis involves extradition law and the interplay of treaties and customary norms. Snowden's asylum-seeking journey, particularly his eventual refuge in Russia, underscored the intricate interface between extradition requests and the concept of political offenses under international law. The diverging interpretations of these legal concepts among states led to diplomatic frictions and laid bare the complexities of navigating legal pathways in cross-border contexts.

Additionally, the disclosures made by Snowden had ramifications for bilateral and multilateral diplomatic relations. Allegations of espionage and breaches of state secrets sparked intense diplomatic tensions between the United States and various other nations. This raised critical questions about the relevance of existing diplomatic protections and the need for recalibrating international understandings in the context of modern information dissemination and cross-border disclosures.

In sum, the international law considerations arising from Edward Snowden's actions transcend traditional boundaries and implicate fundamental precepts of sovereignty, human rights, and diplomatic protocols. As the legal discourse unfolds, it underscores the interconnectedness of global legal frameworks and the imperative of reconciling conflicting interests in a rapidly evolving geopolitical terrain.

Diplomatic Strain: U.S. Relationships on the Global Stage

The revelations brought forth by Edward Snowden introduced a complex diplomatic strain for the United States on the global stage. As sensitive information about surveillance programs and global intelligence operations surfaced, many countries around the world were left grappling with the implications of their relationships with the U.S.

This strain was notably evident in the diplomatic fallout following the disclosure of widespread monitoring activities, prompting widespread concern and critique from international allies and adversaries alike.

Nations such as Germany, Brazil, France, and Mexico expressed outrage at the apparent intrusion into their sovereignty and citizens' privacy. The disclosures led to strained diplomatic relations with these countries, undermining trust and cooperation in various areas, including trade and security partnerships. The U.S. found itself confronting a wave of criticism from foreign leaders and the global community, challenging its credibility and leadership in international affairs.

Furthermore, the diplomatic strain extended to multilateral forums and organizations, where the U.S. traditionally held significant influence. The revelations prompted urgent discussions and debates about privacy rights, cybersecurity, and transparency in international relations. On the global stage, the U.S. faced mounting pressure to address these concerns and reassure its allies of its commitment to upholding mutual respect and adherence to international norms.

The intricate dynamics of diplomatic relationships were further tested as other nations deliberated over how to engage with the U.S. amid ongoing disclosures. Some countries saw an opportunity to assert their own agendas and challenge traditional alliances, while others sought to navigate the delicate balance between pursuing their interests and managing their ties with the U.S. Amidst this backdrop, the U.S. had to carefully navigate diplomatic engagements and negotiations to mitigate the fallout from the Snowden disclosures, fostering a climate of open dialogue and cooperation where possible.

The impact of the diplomatic strain reverberated across numerous spheres, from economic partnerships and defense alliances to intelligence sharing and global governance. It compelled policymakers to reassess their approaches to international engagement and reevaluate the fundamental principles underpinning diplomatic relations. The U.S. found itself embroiled in a delicate dance of addressing the concerns of its global counterparts while reaffirming its commitment to advancing shared interests and upholding collective security and stability.

Extradition Challenges: Legalities and Blockades

The extradition challenges faced by Edward Snowden encapsulate a significant legal battle with profound implications. In the aftermath of the disclosures, the United States government sought to bring Snowden back to American soil to face charges related to espionage and theft of government property. However, the prospect of extradition was fraught with complexities and obstacles.

One of the primary hurdles is the intricate web of extradition laws and treaties between nations. While some countries have strong extradition agreements with the United States, others may harbor legal provisions that prevent the surrender of individuals for certain offenses. This divergence in legal frameworks contributes to the intricacies surrounding Snowden's potential extradition.

Moreover, international public opinion has played a pivotal role in influencing the stance of various governments regarding Snowden's extradition. Advocacy groups, human rights organizations, and public sentiment have contributed to shaping diplomatic discussions and decisions on this matter. Consequently, the balancing act between legal obligations, political considerations, and public support further complicates the extradition process.

Snowden's own circumstances add another layer of complexity to the extradition challenges. As an individual regarded by many as a whistleblower and a defender of civil liberties, his case invokes moral and ethical dimensions that reverberate across international boundaries. The presence of such moral overtones adds nuance to the legal arguments and intensifies the debates around his potential extradition.

Furthermore, Snowden's eventual destination significantly influences the extradition dynamics. His temporary asylum status in Russia has shielded him from immediate extradition to the United States, thereby creating a diplomatic impasse. The geopolitical ramifications of potential extradition further complicate the legal landscape, with implications for bilateral relationships and global politics.

In essence, the extradition challenges pertaining to Edward Snowden epitomize the collision of law, politics, and morality on the international stage. The ongoing developments in this arena continue to shape the discourse surrounding surveillance, whistleblowing, and governmental transparency, making it a crucial facet of contemporary global affairs.

Snowden's Defense and Legal Representation

Edward Snowden's defense and legal representation have been at the center of numerous debates and discussions since the revelations of his actions. As a figure of great controversy, Snowden has relied on a team of skilled attorneys and legal experts to navigate the intricate web of charges and international law. His defense strategy has focused on highlighting the importance of his actions in revealing mass surveillance programs that infringed upon privacy rights and civil liberties.

The legal representation for Snowden has been multifaceted, with lawyers specializing in national security, human rights law, and extradition proceedings coming together to form a formidable team. They have diligently worked to challenge the charges levied against him, employing arguments based on constitutional rights, freedom of speech, and the public interest in exposing government overreach.

One of the key pillars of Snowden's defense has been the assertion that his actions were driven by a moral obligation to inform the public about the extent of government surveillance, rather than a desire for personal gain or malicious intent. His legal team has underscored the global significance of the disclosures and their potential to spark crucial debates about the balance between national security and individual privacy.

Additionally, Snowden's legal representation has continuously engaged with international human rights organizations, legal scholars, and advocacy groups to bolster his defense and garner support for his cause. The collaborative efforts have aimed to shed light on the broader implications of his case beyond the immediate legal ramifications, emphasizing the need for robust protections for whistleblowers and the impact on freedom of expression worldwide.

Despite facing formidable legal challenges, Snowden's defense has steadfastly pursued avenues for legal recourse and fair treatment. This has involved navigating complex extradition procedures, seeking asylum, and advocating for due process in various jurisdictions where his case has resonated. The legal representation has also actively addressed allegations and misconceptions, striving to present a comprehensive and compelling narrative that speaks to the principles underlying Snowden's actions.

As the legal battles continue to unfold, Snowden's defense and legal representation serve as a testament to the enduring significance of his disclosures and the fundamental rights at stake. The ongoing efforts of his legal team reflect a commitment to upholding the values of transparency, accountability, and individual conscience within a framework of legal advocacy and global implications.

Public and Political Pressure on Legal Proceedings

The legal proceedings involving Edward Snowden have been heavily influenced by public and political pressure from both domestic and international stakeholders. The complex nature of the case has attracted widespread attention, leading to various forms of pressure that have significantly impacted the trajectory of legal proceedings. From public opinion to governmental actions, the scrutiny surrounding Snowden's case has had far-reaching implications. A key aspect of this pressure is the division of public sentiment regarding Snowden's actions. While some view him as a courageous whistleblower who exposed government overreach and privacy violations, others perceive him as a traitor who jeopardized national security. This divergence in public perception has led to polarized debates and an intense spotlight on the legal proceedings. Political pressure has also played a pivotal role in shaping the legal landscape for Snowden. Both domestic and foreign governments have exerted influence through diplomatic channels, legal maneuvering, and policy decisions. The United States government, in particular, has faced internal and external pressures regarding its approach to Snowden's case. Domestically, political figures have taken varying stances on the issue, reflecting the broader ideological divisions within the country. Internationally, Snowden's case has strained diplomatic relations between the U.S. and other nations, leading to complex legal and diplomatic intricacies. Furthermore, advocacy groups, civil rights organizations, and prominent public figures have rallied behind Snowden, amplifying the political pressure on legal proceedings. Their vocal support and calls for reform have catalyzed discussions on government transparency, surveillance practices, and the protection of whistleblowers. As a result, the legal framework surrounding Snowden's case has been subject to heightened scrutiny and demands for legal and policy reforms. The interplay between public and political pressure has created a multifaceted backdrop against which legal proceedings unfold. This dynamic environment has posed unique challenges and opportunities within the legal arena, influencing courtroom dynamics, legal strategies, and public discourse. Consequently, the impact of public and political pressure on Snowden's legal proceedings continues to resonate, shaping outcomes and laying the groundwork for broader conversations about accountability, transparency, and the intersection of law and morality.

Potential Outcomes and Consequences

As legal proceedings and diplomatic tensions continue to unfold, the potential outcomes and consequences of Edward Snowden's actions cast a long shadow over the global stage. The resolution of this complex web of legal and diplomatic play will reverberate far beyond Snowden's personal fate, affecting international relations, surveillance policies, and individual rights.

One potential outcome is a landmark legal decision that could redefine the boundaries of government surveillance and whistleblower protections. If Snowden were to stand trial and be found guilty, it could set a precedent for future whistleblowers and dissidents, deterring individuals from exposing government misconduct out of fear of severe repercussions. Conversely, a not-guilty verdict or a favorable legal settlement could signal a shift toward greater transparency and accountability within governmental intelligence agencies.

Moreover, the consequences extend beyond the courtroom, influencing diplomatic relationships between the United States and other nations. The extradition process itself has sparked diplomatic tensions, with countries grappling over their legal obligations, political allegiances, and human rights considerations. The outcome of this process could impact extradition treaties and international cooperation in law enforcement and intelligence-sharing efforts.

In addition to legal and diplomatic implications, the potential outcomes have profound societal and ethical ramifications. Snowden's case has catalyzed public debate on privacy rights, government transparency, and the moral responsibilities of both state actors and private citizens. A finding of guilt may engender disillusionment and erode trust in governmental institutions, while a positive resolution could invigorate a movement toward greater civil liberties and oversight of surveillance programs.

Furthermore, the repercussions of this case may extend into the realm of cybersecurity and digital governance, influencing the development of technologies designed to protect individual privacy and thwart unauthorized surveillance. Innovations in encryption, secure communication networks, and data protection measures may be fueled by the legacy of Snowden's disclosures and the ensuing legal aftermath.

Ultimately, the potential outcomes and consequences of the ongoing legal entanglements are poised to shape the course of history, leaving an indelible mark on the interconnected domains of law, diplomacy, ethics, and technology.

Summarizing the Complex Web of Legal and Diplomatic Play

The intertwining realms of legal charges and diplomatic tensions surrounding Edward Snowden's case create a multifaceted matrix of international implications and intricate legal maneuverings. As Snowden's actions reverberate across borders, a complex web of legal intricacies has emerged, shaping the course of his case and straining diplomatic relations. First and foremost, the potential outcomes and consequences of Snowden's legal entanglements carry significant weight, not only for the individual at the heart of the controversy but also for the broader landscape of national security, civil liberties, and global governance.

The pursuit of Snowden under the Espionage Act has raised critical questions about the balance between national security and government transparency, with far-reaching implications for whistleblower protections and freedom of speech. The historical context and application of the Espionage Act serve as key considerations within this narrative, reflecting the enduring tension between government secrecy and public accountability. This legal backdrop frames the complexity of Snowden's legal predicament and sets the stage for a profound exploration of the intersection between law, morality, and state power.

Furthermore, the U.S. government's reaction and initial charges against Snowden cast a shadow of uncertainty over his future, prompting intense scrutiny of the legal processes and the potential limitations of due process within the national security framework. The very nature of these charges reflects the formidable legal arsenal wielded by the government, fueling debates about the boundaries of legitimate state authority in addressing classified disclosures that challenge the status quo.

In parallel, the international dimension introduces a layer of diplomatic strain that amplifies the scale of Snowden's legal battle. The ramifications of his disclosures have triggered diplomatic tensions, upending traditional alliances and igniting debates on the global stage. Extradition challenges further complicate the legal landscape, with intricate debates surrounding international law, human rights conventions, and extradition treaties shaping the parameters of Snowden's legal defense and international reception.

Amidst this intricate tapestry of legal and diplomatic complexities,

Snowden's defense and legal representation emerge as pivotal elements in navigating the multifaceted web of legal and diplomatic play. The interplay between legal strategies, advocacy efforts, and public perception underscores the dynamic nature of this multidimensional saga, with global implications that extend well beyond the confines of traditional legal proceedings.

Overall, the complex web of legal and diplomatic play encapsulates a convergence of legal arguments, geopolitical dynamics, and ethical considerations, presenting a compelling microcosm of the interwoven nature of international law and statecraft. As the chapter of legal entanglements unfolds, the intricate dance of legal and diplomatic forces propels the narrative forward, unveiling profound insights into the delicate balance of power, justice, and global repercussions.

10

The Aftermath

Immediate Responses from U.S. Government Agencies

In the immediate aftermath of Edward Snowden's disclosures, U.S. government agencies, notably the National Security Agency (NSA) and the Central Intelligence Agency (CIA), scrambled to respond to the seismic impact of the leaks. Within days of the revelations, official statements from these entities sought to reassure the public and address concerns about the implications for national security. Both agencies released press releases acknowledging the leaks while emphasizing the legality and necessity of their surveillance programs in safeguarding the country from external threats. These statements formed a crucial part of the government's initial damage control efforts, attempting to balance transparency with maintaining the perceived integrity of their operations.

Concurrently, immediate security measures were taken within these agencies to address potential vulnerabilities arising from the disclosed information. There was heightened internal scrutiny, as well as reviews and assessments of existing protocols and security clearance procedures. The very nature of their operations necessitated swift responses to mitigate any perceived risks to ongoing intelligence operations and personnel safety.

Beyond official communications, there were visible shifts in the conduct and visibility of these agencies. Increased interactions with the media, attempts to provide more insight into their activities while safeguarding classified information, and engaging with stakeholders all contributed to an evolving narrative around the role and accountability of government surveillance programs. It was a period of significant introspection and reevaluation, both internally and in terms of external communications.

The stance taken by the U.S. government agencies in the wake of the disclosures became integral to shaping subsequent responses and influencing public perceptions. This phase marked the beginning of a dynamic interplay between transparency, security imperatives, and the complex relationship between the government and its citizens.

Impact on U.S. Foreign Relations

Edward Snowden's disclosures about the U.S. government's extensive surveillance programs had a profound impact on U.S. foreign relations. The revelations of widespread spying on foreign governments, including key allies such as Germany, Brazil, and Mexico, led to a significant erosion of trust and strained diplomatic relationships. The exposed activities caused outrage and condemnation among foreign leaders and citizens alike, with allegations of breaches of international law and infringement on privacy rights. As a result, the U.S. faced increased scrutiny and criticism on the global stage. Nations that were targeted by U.S. surveillance operations demanded explanations, apologies, and assurances that such actions would not be repeated. This tumultuous period witnessed diplomatic tensions, strained alliances, and a reassessment of international partnerships. The revelations also prompted some countries to take defensive measures to protect their communications and data from potential U.S. espionage, leading to shifts in trade, intelligence sharing, and security cooperation agreements. The fallout from the disclosures reverberated across the global landscape, affecting the U.S.'s standing and influence in international affairs. To mitigate the damage, the U.S. government engaged in diplomatic efforts to mend fractured relationships and rebuild trust with affected nations, acknowledging the need for transparency and accountability. However, the lingering repercussions of the surveillance scandal continued to cast a shadow over U.S. foreign policy and its interactions with other countries, reshaping the dynamics of international diplomacy and raising new challenges for diplomacy and national security.

Changes in National Security Protocols

Following the unprecedented revelations brought to light by Edward Snowden, the United States underwent a significant reassessment of its national security protocols and intelligence gathering methods. The disclosures triggered a nationwide debate on the boundaries between security and privacy, leading to a critical examination of existing surveillance programs. As a response to the public outcry and concerns regarding mass surveillance, there was a notable shift in the approach to national security protocols.

One of the most substantial changes was the introduction of reform initiatives aimed at increasing transparency and oversight within the intelligence community. The government implemented measures to enhance accountability and establish stricter guidelines for the collection and analysis of data. Additionally, efforts were made to limit the scope of bulk metadata collection, balancing the imperative to safeguard national security with the protection of individual privacy rights. These developments represented a marked departure from the previously secretive nature of surveillance operations.

Moreover, there was an emphasis on reinforcing the vetting processes for individuals granted access to classified information. This included bolstering security clearance procedures and implementing stringent safeguards to prevent unauthorized disclosures. The priority became cultivating a culture of responsibility and integrity among personnel with access to sensitive intelligence, thereby mitigating the risk of further leaks.

The recalibration of national security protocols also extended to the technological realm, where extensive efforts were made to fortify cybersecurity defenses and safeguard critical infrastructure. Collaboration between government agencies and private sector entities intensified, fostering a collective endeavor to combat cyber threats and strengthen resilience against potential breaches.

Simultaneously, there was a concerted push for increased judicial oversight and more rigorous scrutiny of surveillance activities. Judicial review mechanisms were refined to provide thorough assessments of surveillance requests, ensuring that the legal framework governing intelligence operations remained consistent with constitutional principles and statutory regulations.

Overall, the aftermath of Edward Snowden's disclosures precipitated a profound rethinking of national security protocols in the United States. The paradigm shift towards greater transparency, accountability, and adherence to legal boundaries sought to reconcile the imperatives of national security with the imperative of respecting civil liberties and individual privacy, setting the stage for a new era in the nation's approach to intelligence gathering and protection.

Media Coverage and Public Opinion Shifts

The publication of the leaked documents by Edward Snowden triggered a seismic shift in media coverage and public opinion on matters relating to government surveillance and individual privacy. Initially, the revelations sparked intense debate and scrutiny across various media platforms, drawing attention from traditional news outlets to social media forums. The story dominated headlines, with experts analyzing the implications while the public grappled with the concept of widespread government monitoring. The unprecedented nature of the disclosures led to a frenzy of reporting, as journalists delved into the specifics of the surveillance programs, uncovering their far-reaching scope and potential impact on civil liberties. This resulted in heightened public awareness and concern, manifesting in significant shifts in public opinion concerning privacy and security. As more information came to light, citizens began re-evaluating their trust in government institutions and critically examining the balance between national security and personal freedoms. Additionally, international media coverage broadened the discourse, fostering global conversations about the implications of mass surveillance and the conduct of world powers. The pervasive coverage also intersected with political agendas, shaping public sentiment and influencing policy debates at local and international levels. The convergence of media coverage and evolving public opinion ultimately catalyzed legislative and regulatory discussions, compelling governments to address the concerns and demands of their constituents. In essence, the media played a pivotal role in shaping the aftermath of the Snowden revelations, acting as a catalyst for public opinion shifts and prompting a reconsideration of privacy rights and government accountability.

Technology Companies' Reactions and Policy Changes

In the wake of Edward Snowden's disclosures, technology companies around the globe faced a significant ethical and operational quandary. Their products and services were critical components in the surveillance programs revealed by Snowden, raising profound questions about their complicity in enabling government overreach. This pivotal moment compelled these tech giants to reevaluate their roles in safeguarding user privacy and data protection. In response to the revelations, numerous technology companies initiated comprehensive reviews of their internal policies and practices, striving to reinforce transparency and accountability. They endeavored to enhance encryption measures, fortify cybersecurity protocols, and intensify resistance against unwarranted government intrusion. Notably, this shift resonated across industry leaders, as they sought to rebuild public trust and restore confidence in their commitment to privacy rights. As a result, many corporations instituted sweeping policy changes, rejecting indiscriminate data collection and advocating for stronger legal protections for their users. Amid mounting public concerns, these companies proactively engaged in dialogue with policymakers, advocating for reforms that would curb mass surveillance while still addressing legitimate national security imperatives. Additionally, some technology firms collaborated with civil liberties organizations, contributing to the development of pivotal legal precedents and landmark legislation regarding government data access and transparency. The aftermath of Snowden's disclosures thus catalyzed a paradigm shift within the technology sector, prompting a movement towards greater corporate responsibility and principled advocacy. Ultimately, the impact of technology companies' reactions and policy changes transcended organizational boundaries, permeating global conversations about digital rights, personal privacy, and the balance between security and individual freedoms.

Legislative Responses and Discussions

In the aftermath of Edward Snowden's revelations, the legislative landscape underwent a significant transformation as lawmakers grappled with the implications of mass surveillance programs. The disclosures sparked intense debate within both houses of Congress, leading to the introduction of various bills aimed at reforming existing surveillance laws and enhancing privacy protections for citizens. Key legislators from different political factions engaged in heated discussions on the appropriate balance between national security imperatives and individual privacy rights. This tumultuous period saw the emergence of bipartisan alliances advocating for increased transparency and oversight of intelligence activities.

One of the pivotal moments came with the introduction of the USA FREEDOM Act, a comprehensive legislation designed to curtail the bulk collection of telecommunication metadata by the National Security

Agency (NSA). The bill drew support from a diverse coalition of civil liberties advocates, technology companies, and concerned citizens who viewed it as a critical step towards reining in government overreach in the digital era. However, its passage was not without fierce opposition from proponents of the status quo, who argued that stringent measures could undermine the nation's counterterrorism efforts.

While the USA FREEDOM Act ultimately became law, its provisions triggered ongoing deliberations surrounding the broader scope of surveillance reform. Lawmakers continued to engage in deliberations concerning the renewal of controversial provisions of the Foreign Intelligence Surveillance Act (FISA), prompting contentious negotiations and floor debates. Simultaneously, committees convened hearings that scrutinized the efficacy of existing oversight mechanisms and explored avenues for bolstering accountability within the intelligence community.

The discourse surrounding legislative responses to Snowden's disclosures also extended beyond Capitol Hill, manifesting in public forums, academic symposiums, and legal conferences nationwide. Notably, prominent constitutional scholars and legal experts contributed to the discourse by publishing influential analyses and participating in constitutional challenges against intrusive surveillance practices. These concerted efforts propelled the issue into the forefront of the national consciousness, galvanizing widespread interest and mobilizing citizens to demand greater protections for their digital privacy.

Furthermore, the global reverberations of Snowden's revelations prompted discussions on the interplay between domestic laws and international human rights standards. Legislators sought to harmonize U.S. surveillance activities with international norms, fostering dialogues with foreign counterparts and multilateral organizations to address cross-border data privacy concerns. This engagement underscored the interconnected nature of global surveillance practices and underscored the need for collaborative frameworks that uphold fundamental rights while safeguarding legitimate security interests.

The legislative responses and discussions catalyzed by Snowden's disclosures constituted a watershed moment in the ongoing evolution of surveillance policy, marking a paradigm shift in the dynamics between government authority and individual privacy. This chapter of history reflects the enduring impact of a single individual's actions in igniting a transformative reevaluation of democratic principles in the digital age.

Effects on Privacy Advocacy Groups

In the wake of Edward Snowden's revelations about mass surveillance programs conducted by the U.S. government, privacy advocacy groups experienced a seismic shift in their operations and strategies. The exposure of extensive data collection and monitoring activities raised profound concerns about privacy rights, civil liberties, and the balance between national security and individual freedoms. Privacy advocacy groups found themselves thrust into the spotlight, prompting a reevaluation of their roles and influence in shaping public discourse and policy decisions. Amidst the tumultuous aftermath of Snowden's disclosures, these organizations became central players in advocating for greater transparency, accountability, and legal reforms within the surveillance landscape.

One of the immediate effects on privacy advocacy groups was a surge in public engagement and support. Snowden's revelations galvanized individuals and communities around the world, sparking widespread discussions on privacy, government oversight, and the implications of pervasive surveillance. This heightened public awareness provided advocacy groups with a larger platform to amplify their messages and mobilize grassroots efforts. They leveraged this momentum to champion privacy rights through educational campaigns, public demonstrations, and collaborations with other civil society organizations dedicated to safeguarding individual privacy.

Moreover, the disclosures catalyzed a reexamination of existing legislative frameworks and spurred advocacy groups to intensify their lobbying efforts. These organizations actively participated in legislative hearings, policy debates, and legal challenges aimed at enhancing privacy protections and curtailing unchecked government surveillance powers. Their expertise and evidence-based advocacy bolstered the drive for meaningful policy reforms, resulting in proposals for increased oversight, data transparency, and judicial review of surveillance activities. As a result, privacy advocacy groups played a pivotal role in shaping the discourse surrounding government surveillance practices and compelling lawmakers to consider the broader societal implications of their decisions.

Furthermore, the fallout from Snowden's revelations prompted privacy advocacy groups to embrace technological innovation as a means to fortify digital privacy and security. Recognizing the critical role of encryption technologies and digital hygiene practices in thwarting unwarranted intrusions, these organizations dedicated resources to advancing secure communication tools, promoting encryption literacy, and empowering individuals to safeguard their online activities. By equipping the public with knowledge and tools to protect their digital footprints, privacy advocates sought to counteract the chilling effects of pervasive surveillance and foster a climate of empowerment amidst growing concerns about privacy erosion.

In addition to shaping public opinion and legislative momentum, privacy advocacy groups faced heightened scrutiny and challenges from adversaries seeking to undermine their efforts. Critics questioned the motives and allegiances of these organizations, portraying them as impediments to national security or trivializing their concerns as alarmist. Despite these obstacles, privacy advocacy groups remained resolute in their commitment to upholding privacy as a fundamental human right and pushing back against overreaching surveillance practices. They navigated complex legal and political landscapes while engaging in constructive dialogues with stakeholders across diverse sectors to advance their cause.

Ultimately, the impact of Edward Snowden's disclosures reverberated throughout the privacy advocacy landscape, sparking a period of introspection, mobilization, and evolution. Privacy advocacy groups emerged from this transformative chapter with heightened visibility, bolstered advocacy strategies, and a renewed sense of purpose in safeguarding digital privacy and civil liberties in the face of unprecedented surveillance challenges.

Snowden's Personal Circumstances Post-Leak

Following the seismic fallout from the release of classified information, Edward Snowden found himself embroiled in a situation that transcended the realms of traditional whistleblowing. His decision to disclose sensitive government data fundamentally altered the course of his personal and professional life. In the aftermath of the leaks, Snowden faced unprecedented challenges on both legal and personal fronts. Living in exile in Russia, he grappled with the complexities of navigating life away from his home country while being a focal point of global attention. The repercussions of his actions extended beyond the political realm, seeping into the very fabric of his everyday existence. Snowden's personal life became inexorably entwined with the ramifications of his controversial disclosures. The strain of living with the knowledge of potential legal consequences, coupled with constant scrutiny from international media, undoubtedly took a toll on his wellbeing. Furthermore, the rift created within his familial relationships as a result of his choices added an additional layer of complexity to his post-leak circumstances. Despite the challenges, Snowden remained committed to advocating for his beliefs and principles. His stance on civil liberties, government transparency, and individual privacy continued to shape his decisions and interactions in the wake of the whistleblowing episode. This period post-leak marked a profound transition in Snowden's personal narrative, illuminating the intersection between an individual's moral conviction and the far-reaching implications of their actions.

Evaluation of U.S. Surveillance Tactics Post-Aftermath

Following the unprecedented disclosures made by Edward Snowden, the evaluation of U.S. surveillance tactics has become a critical focal point for governmental and public scrutiny alike. The aftermath of these revelations prompted a reexamination of the balance between national security imperatives and individual privacy rights.

In the wake of Snowden's disclosures, there was a discernible shift in how the American public viewed the government's surveillance tactics. This seismic shift in public sentiment sparked an urgent need to assess the legitimacy and necessity of such expansive surveillance programs. The revelation of mass data collection programs, such as the NSA's bulk metadata collection, triggered widespread concerns about the overreach of government surveillance and its potential adverse impact on civil liberties.

This reevaluation of surveillance tactics also extended to the legislative and judicial realms. The revelations propelled profound and long-overdue debates within legislative bodies regarding the oversight and regulation of intelligence agencies' surveillance activities. Additionally, they catalyzed legal challenges that questioned the constitutionality and legality of certain surveillance practices, eventually leading to significant rulings and reforms.

Moreover, the global reverberations of Snowden's disclosures necessitated a comprehensive reassessment of U.S. surveillance tactics in the international arena. The strained diplomatic relations resulting from the disclosure of covert surveillance operations underscored the far-reaching implications of unfettered intelligence gathering on both domestic and foreign policy fronts. Furthermore, the ethical and strategic implications of such revelations had broad repercussions on the global stage, impacting alliances, trust, and international cooperation.

In response to the tumultuous aftermath of the disclosures, technology companies also undertook a thorough review of their involvement in government surveillance initiatives. The complicity of major tech firms in facilitating data extraction and intelligence-gathering efforts raised fundamental ethical and corporate responsibility questions, prompting substantial reform and heightened advocacy for user privacy protection.

The evaluation of U.S. surveillance tactics post-aftermath stands as a pivotal juncture in the ongoing discourse concerning the delicate equilibrium between security imperatives and civil liberties. The fallout from Snowden's revelations precipitated a profound reevaluation of governmental policies, legal frameworks, societal attitudes, and global dynamics, shaping the trajectory of surveillance practices and their enduring implications.

Reflections on the State of Whistleblowing

The aftermath of Edward Snowden's disclosures has prompted deep reflections on the state of whistleblowing, revealing the complex interplay between government transparency, national security, and individual freedoms. As the public grapples with the implications of Snowden's actions, it becomes imperative to consider how the concept of whistleblowing has evolved within contemporary society.

Whistleblowing, a fundamental aspect of organizational oversight and accountability, has historically been met with both praise and condemnation. The Snowden case has reinvigorated discussions around the moral and legal obligations of individuals exposing classified information in the public interest. Debates have intensified regarding the role of whistleblowers in shaping public discourse, challenging governmental secrecy, and safeguarding democratic principles.

One crucial aspect deserving reflection is the impact of technological advancements on the practice of whistleblowing. The proliferation of digital surveillance tools, coupled with heightened security measures, presents unprecedented challenges for individuals seeking to expose misconduct or abuse of power within powerful institutions. As a result, whistleblowers like Snowden are hailed as catalysts for transparency while simultaneously facing severe repercussions for their actions, sparking poignant discussions about the balance between national security and civil liberties.

Furthermore, Snowden's case has brought attention to the role of media and its capacity to amplify the voices of whistleblowers. The dynamic relationship between journalists and whistleblowers reflects an intricate dance between freedom of the press and the responsibilities of protecting sensitive information. The ethical considerations surrounding the publication of classified materials continue to be scrutinized, highlighting the need for nuanced approaches in disseminating crucial information without compromising security or endangering lives.

In essence, these reflections underscore the evolving landscape of whistleblowing in modern society, prompting a critical reevaluation of the mechanisms designed to protect those who seek to shed light on wrongdoing. As Snowden's legacy continues to shape global conversations, it is evident that the state of whistleblowing stands at a crossroads, demanding comprehensive dialogue and ethical deliberation to navigate the delicate balance between transparency and national security.

11

Asylum Seeking: Snowden's Escape and Exile in Russia

Precipitating Factors: Why Russia?

Following Edward Snowden's dramatic departure from Hong Kong in June 2013, the world watched with bated breath as he sought refuge amidst an international manhunt. His decision to turn to Russia for asylum, rather than other potentially sympathetic nations, sparked fervent debate and speculation. The choice of Russia as a temporary haven can be attributed to a complex interplay of personal safety considerations and geopolitical calculations. Firstly, given his predicament as a wanted figure by the United States government, Snowden needed to seek refuge in a country that could offer robust protection from extradition and legal prosecution. Russia, with its strained relationship with the U.S. and a history of granting asylum to high-profile defectors, emerged as a viable option for safeguarding Snowden from facing immediate arrest and extradition. Furthermore, the geopolitical dimension cannot be overlooked. Russia's contentious relationship with the United States lent significant weight to Snowden's decision. By sheltering him, Russia had the opportunity to score diplomatic points against its adversary, challenging the U.S.'s moral high ground and signaling defiance against American global influence. This move served to amplify the international publicity surrounding Snowden's case and exert further pressure on U.S.-Russia relations. Moreover, considering the strategic interests at play, the prospect of gaining access to Snowden's trove of classified information may have been an enticing factor for Russian authorities. This aligns with historical instances where Russia has welcomed defectors in exchange for intelligence assets. Such considerations underscore the multifaceted rationale behind Snowden's choice of Russia as his destination. While his decision was not devoid of controversy and criticism, it represented a calculated move shaped by a blend of personal safety imperatives and strategic geopolitical positioning.

Timeline of Escape: From Hong Kong to Moscow

Edward Snowden's journey from Hong Kong to Moscow in 2013 was a riveting series of events that captured global attention and raised profound questions about international relations, surveillance, and individual rights. The timeline of this escape is rife with intrigue and controversy, illuminating the complexities of modern geopolitics and the power dynamics at play. It all began with Snowden's decision to reveal classified documents on the United States government's surveillance programs. Fearing repercussions and seeking sanctuary, he fled to Hong Kong, where he met with journalists and shared his trove of sensitive information. As the U.S. government sought his extradition, Snowden faced a tense and uncertain period, navigating legal and diplomatic obstacles. His movements were closely monitored by the media and the public, as speculation swirled about his next destination. With mounting pressure and looming threats of arrest, Snowden departed Hong Kong, embarking on a precarious odyssey with far-reaching implications. His transit through various countries, as he sought asylum or safe passage, underscored the immense stakes involved in his quest for liberty and protection. Ultimately, after a dramatic and suspenseful sequence of events, Snowden found temporary refuge in Russia, where he remains to this day. The intricate details of the timeline shed light on the intricacies of international law, state sovereignty, and humanitarian considerations. This chapter will delve into the complexities and significance of each twist and turn in Snowden's perilous journey, offering a comprehensive analysis of the multifaceted factors that shaped his escape and subsequent asylum in Russia.

Diplomatic Dynamics: U.S. Reactions and Requests

In the aftermath of Edward Snowden's arrival in Moscow, the diplomatic arena became a battleground for competing interests and demands. The United States, upon learning of Snowden's presence in Russia, swiftly reacted with a forceful stance, demanding his immediate extradition to face charges related to espionage and theft of government property. This development strained the already complex relationship between the two nations, escalating tensions and reshaping the international landscape.

The U.S. government's requests for Russia to hand over Snowden intensified as it viewed his actions as detrimental to national security and perceived him as a fugitive from justice. This put significant pressure on Russia, prompting a delicate diplomatic dance defined by legal intricacies and geopolitical implications.

As the U.S. exerted considerable effort to secure Snowden's return, the Russian government faced a crucial decision that extended beyond bilateral relations. With global attention fixated on the unfolding saga, Russia found itself at the center of a high-stakes geopolitical standoff, scrutinized for both its handling of asylum requests and its willingness to challenge U.S. authority.

Amidst the mounting pressure, Russia's response was calculated and strategic, leveraging the situation to assert its own political agenda while also carefully considering the potential impact on international partnerships and alliances. The standoff underscored the complexities of modern diplomacy, illustrating how individual cases can have far-reaching consequences for global politics and power dynamics.

Simultaneously, the case exposed the limitations of traditional diplomatic channels in an era defined by rapid information dissemination and evolving public opinions. The U.S. government's efforts to navigate this multifaceted crisis exemplified the intricate interplay between legal, ethical, and strategic considerations, illuminating the challenges inherent in addressing high-profile cases that capture international attention.

Ultimately, the diplomatic discourse surrounding Snowden's asylum in Russia served as a microcosm of broader geopolitical shifts, showcasing the intricate web of intertwined interests, legal frameworks, and power dynamics that dictate the course of international relations in the contemporary world.

Legal Limbo: International Law and Asylum Rights

In the complex web of international law, asylum rights have emerged as a contentious issue in the context of Edward Snowden's exile in Russia. The legal limbo surrounding Snowden's asylum status raises fundamental questions about the rights and obligations of both individuals and states within the framework of international law. At the core of this debate lies the tension between national security concerns and the protection of whistleblowers. International law provides a set of guidelines for the granting of asylum, which hinges on the principle of non-refoulement - the prohibition of returning a refugee to a country where they may face persecution. However, the interpretation and application of these principles differ across jurisdictions, contributing to the legal uncertainty that characterizes Snowden's situation. Snowden's case has reignited discussions about the balance between national security imperatives and the protection of individuals seeking asylum. The interplay of diplomatic relations, human rights considerations, and geopolitical interests further complicates the legal landscape. The evolving nature of technology and global interconnectedness has added new dimensions to the asylum discourse, as evidenced by the prevalence of transnational surveillance practices. This has prompted calls for an updated legal framework that addresses the implications of technological advancements on individual privacy and freedom. At the heart of the legal limbo surrounding Snowden's asylum is the broader question of how international law adapts to accommodate the evolving complexities of contemporary geopolitics and the responsibilities of states towards individuals who expose wrongdoing. With diverging interpretations and applications of asylum laws, the legal limbo surrounding Snowden's asylum status is emblematic of the challenges inherent in reconciling national security concerns with the protection of human rights. In light of this, Snowden's case serves as a catalyst for reevaluating and potentially reforming the international legal framework governing asylum rights, laying bare the need for a nuanced and responsive approach to the intersection of law, ethics, and global security.

Life in Exile: Daily Realities for Snowden in Russia

Edward Snowden's decision to seek asylum in Russia was a significant turning point in his journey as a whistleblower. As he settled into his new life in exile, he encountered a complex set of daily realities that would come to define his existence in this unfamiliar environment. Living under the protection of Russian authorities, Snowden faced numerous challenges and adjustments as he navigated the legal, societal, and personal dimensions of his new reality. The contours of his daily life in Russia were shaped by a delicate balance of security, limited freedom of movement, and enduring scrutiny from international media and intelligence agencies. Despite being granted temporary asylum, Snowden had to adapt to the constraints of his circumstances, mindful of the political and diplomatic sensitivities surrounding his presence in Russia. On a personal level, he had to grapple with the emotional strain of being separated from his home country and loved ones, while attempting to forge meaningful connections with a support network in Russia. Navigating the intricacies of daily life, including mundane tasks such as grocery shopping, attending to administrative matters, and ensuring his personal safety, posed constant challenges. Each day brought both opportunities and obstacles, as Snowden sought to maintain a sense of purpose and normalcy amidst the extraordinary circumstances of his exile. Moreover, the psychological and emotional impact of existing in a state of limbo, uncertain about his long-term prospects, weighed heavily on his mind. This period of his life was marked by a profound sense of isolation and uncertainty, as he grappled with the implications of his choices and the ramifications for his future. Amidst this tumultuous backdrop, Snowden found moments of solace and solidarity with those who empathized with his predicament. His daily realities in Russia were a compelling juxtaposition of resilience and vulnerability, as he confronted the multifaceted implications of his status as a whistleblower in exile. As time passed, the daily rhythms of life in Russia became intertwined with the broader narrative of Snowden's ongoing impact on global conversations around surveillance, privacy, and governmental transparency.

Russian Motivations: Strategic Interests and Human Rights

As Edward Snowden sought asylum in Russia following his high-profile disclosure of classified information, the decision made by the Russian government to offer refuge to him was influenced by a complex interplay of strategic interests and considerations related to human rights. At the core of Russia's motivations was the opportunity to leverage Snowden's presence for its own geopolitical advantage. By granting asylum to Snowden, Russia aimed to demonstrate its autonomy and assert itself as a defender of individuals persecuted by Western powers. This move aligned with Russia's broader strategy of challenging the global dominance of the United States and positioning itself as a counterforce on the world stage. Moreover, sheltering Snowden allowed Russia to castigate the U.S. on matters of human rights and civil liberties, thereby bolstering its international image and influence. From a strategic standpoint, providing sanctuary to Snowden also presented an opportunity for Russia to glean insights from the trove of sensitive information he possessed, potentially enhancing its own intelligence capabilities and geopolitical maneuvering. Beyond these strategic calculations, the decision to accommodate Snowden resonated with elements of human rights diplomacy in Russian foreign policy. By harboring a prominent whistleblower like Snowden, the Russian government could project an image of championing dissent and individual freedoms, especially in contrast to what it portrayed as the repressive practices of the U.S. and its allies. This narrative enabled Russia to present itself as a beacon of refuge for those facing persecution or censorship in other parts of the world, aligning with its efforts to position itself as a proponent of global human rights protection. However, it is important to note that while offering asylum to Snowden served Russia's strategic interests and projected an image of upholding human rights, it also raised criticisms regarding Russia's own record on civil liberties and freedom of expression. This dichotomy underscored the complexity and multifaceted nature of Russia's motivations in sheltering Edward Snowden amidst the backdrop of strategic calculations and human rights posturing.

Media Portrayal: Coverage of Snowden's Russian Asylum

The media portrayal of Edward Snowden's asylum in Russia has been a subject of intense scrutiny and debate. The coverage by various news outlets, both domestically and internationally, has reflected diverse perspectives, from depicting Snowden as a hero to casting him as a traitor. This section delves into the nuanced lens through which the media has depicted Snowden's life in Russian exile. In the immediate aftermath of Snowden's arrival in Russia, media attention was fervently focused on the circumstances surrounding his sudden presence in the country. Speculations and analyses regarding the implications of Russia providing asylum to the whistleblower dominated headlines across the globe.The dichotomy in portrayal was stark, with some media outlets framing Russia's decision as a bold stance for freedom of speech and human rights, while others characterized it as a calculated geopolitical maneuver against the United States. In the ensuing years, the media's coverage of Snowden's life in Russia has intertwined with broader narratives about surveillance, privacy, and government transparency. It has often featured interviews with Snowden conducted by journalists granted access to him in Moscow. Moreover, media reports have chronicled the challenges faced by Snowden in adapting to a vastly different cultural and political environment, shedding light on the personal toll of his exile. Furthermore, speculation about Russia's treatment of Snowden, ranging from speculations of surveillance to questions about his degree of freedom, has perpetuated a continuous stream of interest and analysis. The evolving nature of the media's narrative around Snowden's presence in Russia has influenced public perceptions and played a critical role in shaping the ongoing discourse surrounding surveillance, national security, and individual liberties. It has also engendered debates about the media's role in influencing the public's understanding of contentious issues and the intersection of journalism, politics, and global diplomacy. As such, the media's portrayal of Snowden's Russian asylum has had enduring significance in the broader contexts of international relations and civil liberties, sparking conversations about the responsibilities and ethical considerations of media organizations in covering sensitive and geopolitically charged subjects.

Implications for U.S.-Russia Relations

The asylum granted to Edward Snowden in Russia established a significant point of contention between the United States and Russia, reshaping their diplomatic relations and adding layers of complexity to their interactions. The decision by Russian authorities to provide refuge to Snowden had immediate and enduring implications for bilateral ties, injecting fresh tension into an already strained relationship. From the perspective of the United States, Snowden's presence in Russia was perceived as more than just an individual case; it represented a direct challenge to U.S. authority and posed a grave threat to national security. This move strained existing trust between the two nations and amplified suspicions on both sides. Moreover, the U.S. government's vocal objections to Russia's decision heightened the diplomatic friction, leading to a series of retaliatory measures and strained negotiations.

The Snowden affair also deepened pre-existing fault lines in the realms of human rights, extradition policies, and privacy laws. The stark divergence in perspectives on these issues between the United States and Russia placed additional strain on their relations, with each side criticizing the other's stance and actions. This divergence pushed the bilateral relationship into a new phase characterized by increased diplomatic back-and-forth, mutual recriminations, and diverging narratives presented to the global community.

In addition to the immediate effects on bilateral interactions, the asylum granted to Snowden in Russia triggered broader geopolitical implications that extended beyond the U.S.-Russia relationship. The event became a focal point for international analysis and debate, drawing attention to the shifting power dynamics and alliances in the global arena. It reinvigorated discussions about the contrasting approaches to governance, surveillance, and freedom between the United States and Russia, exposing fundamental differences in values, priorities, and strategies.

Despite the substantial strains caused by the Snowden asylum issue, there were also instances where the U.S.-Russia relations found common ground. These moments, albeit rare, provided glimpses of potential areas for cooperation amidst the discord. Both countries continued engagement on certain regional and global issues, demonstrating a degree of pragmatism alongside the confrontational dynamics. However, the lingering shadow of the Snowden saga remained, influencing the conduct of diplomacy and shaping the contours of broader strategic calculations.

As the implications of Snowden's presence in Russia reverberated in the realm of international relations, they served as a stark reminder of the interconnectedness and interdependence of modern geopolitical actors. The standoff over Snowden propelled the U.S.-Russia relationship into a new chapter characterized by heightened scrutiny, mutual suspicion, and strategic recalibrations. While the long-term consequences remained uncertain, the impact of this episode underscored the far-reaching implications of individual acts on the broader tapestry of global politics.

Snowden's Communications: Statements and Interviews from Exile

Amidst the shadow of exile, Edward Snowden maintained a presence in the public sphere through a series of carefully crafted statements and interviews. His communications from Russia offered a window into his evolving perspectives, motivations, and steadfast commitment to the cause of privacy rights. Despite the geographic distance, Snowden's words resonated globally, igniting debates and shaping narratives that extended far beyond the boundaries of his temporary refuge. Each communication was meticulously orchestrated, bearing the weight of both personal conviction and calculated strategy. These messages served as beacons of insight, conveying not only his individual experiences but also universal truths about power, surveillance, and freedom. Snowden emerged as a formidable voice, leveraging technology and media to deliver his potent message. From poignant essays to thought-provoking interviews, each instance of communication exemplified Snowden's unwavering dedication to transparency and dissent. Whether addressing global parliaments or engaging with journalists, his eloquence and principled stance reinforced the enduring impact of his disclosures. The resonance of his exile reverberated throughout the digital realm, encapsulating the dichotomy of restriction and liberation. While physically confined by geopolitical circumstance, Snowden's digital presence transcended borders, circumventing conventional forms of control.

Those who sought to silence him inadvertently amplified his narrative, leading to heightened attention on the issues at the core of his actions. Snowden's communications catalyzed collective introspection and challenged constituents of power, prompting individuals and institutions to confront the complexities of governance, accountability, and civil liberties. Within each carefully chosen word, the spirit of injustice confronted and the insistence on ethical rectitude remained resolute.

Future Prospects: Potential Scenarios for Snowden's Status

As Edward Snowden continues his exile in Russia, the potential scenarios for his status hold great significance and uncertainty. The complex web of international politics, legal considerations, and public opinion creates a landscape of possibilities as Snowden navigates this chapter of his life.

One potential scenario is the prospect of a presidential pardon or clemency from the United States government. Advocates have called for such measures, arguing that Snowden's actions served to expose significant governmental overreach and surveillance abuses, sparking vital conversations about privacy rights and civil liberties. However, with various U.S. officials categorizing Snowden's actions as treasonous, the likelihood of official pardons remains uncertain.

Another possible trajectory for Snowden's future involves seeking formal asylum in other countries. As dynamics in global politics evolve, Snowden may explore options beyond his current place of residence. This could involve diplomatic negotiations, legal deliberations, and assessments of geopolitical implications for both host nations and the United States. It presents a complex and multifaceted process that intertwines legal, political, and humanitarian dimensions.

Furthermore, the ongoing debate over Snowden's legacy and the impact of his disclosures continues to shape the prospects for his status. Public sentiment and evolving attitudes toward privacy, security, and whistleblowing play a pivotal role in influencing the trajectory of Snowden's future. This includes considerations of how historical narratives may reflect on his actions and their long-term implications for societal values and governance.

Moreover, the potential enacting of whistleblower protections and reform within the U.S. legal framework could impact Snowden's future outlook. These legislative developments may alter the landscape for individuals who seek to expose misconduct within governmental organizations, thereby influencing the incentives and deterrents relevant to Snowden's circumstances.

Finally, the broader global context and shifts in international relations have the potential to impact Snowden's status. Geopolitical realignments, changes in diplomatic dynamics, and evolving norms regarding asylum and extradition carry substantive implications for Snowden's situation. As global power dynamics ebb and flow, so too does the terrain upon which Snowden's future prospects are drawn.

These potential scenarios for Snowden's status intertwine a myriad of legal, political, and ethical considerations. As Snowden continues to navigate his exile in Russia, these factors form the backdrop against which his future may unfold.

12

Global Impact

Global Repercussions

The revelations of Edward Snowden's leaks in 2013 stirred a maelstrom of reactions across the global political landscape. Governments and leaders worldwide were compelled to confront the startling implications of the disclosed NSA surveillance programs. The initial response was marked by a mixture of shock, outrage, and a profound sense of betrayal among allies and adversaries alike. This unprecedented breach of trust gave rise to an urgent need for reassessment and recalibration of international relations, with security and privacy concerns at the forefront. As the news reverberated around the world, it catalyzed a seismic shift in how nations approached data security, foreign policy, and diplomatic engagements. These early responses set the tone for ongoing dialogues, cooperation, and contention on a global scale, shaping the contours of contemporary geopolitics. The significance of these initial reactions lies not only in their immediate impact but also in their enduring influence on the evolving landscape of international relations in the digital age. The subsequent chapters delve deeper into the specific repercussions stemming from these seminal moments, elucidating the lasting effects and far-reaching consequences of Snowden's disclosures on the international stage.

Reactions from International Governments

As news of Edward Snowden's revelations reverberated around the world, governments across the globe were confronted with the seismic impact of his disclosures. The reactions from international governments varied greatly, reflecting the unique geopolitical considerations, diplomatic relationships, and national security priorities of each country. In response to the startling revelations, some governments expressed outrage, viewing Snowden's actions as a direct challenge to their intelligence operations and a breach of trust in international relations. This led to strained diplomatic relations between the United States and several nations, as allegations surfaced regarding the extent of U.S. surveillance activities on foreign soil. Conversely, other countries seized the opportunity to amplify their own concerns about privacy violations and espionage, using Snowden's disclosures as leverage to call for greater transparency and accountability in global surveillance practices.

Furthermore, the reactions from international governments had profound implications for multilateral relations and cooperation in counterterrorism efforts. The revelations ignited debates within various international forums and organizations, leading to discussions about the need for revised norms and regulations governing intelligence sharing and data collection between nations. Some governments recognized the urgency of recalibrating their surveillance policies and enhancing safeguards against unwarranted intrusion into citizens' private communications and online activities. This catalyzed collaborative efforts aimed at reevaluating existing agreements and bilateral treaties related to intelligence-sharing activities among partner countries.

Additionally, the global response to Snowden's disclosures underscored significant disparities in public attitudes toward government surveillance and privacy rights. While nations with robust traditions of civil liberties and constitutional protections saw mounting calls for increased oversight and judicial review of intelligence gathering, other countries with authoritarian regimes sought to capitalize on the perceived vulnerabilities exposed by the leaks, deepening their monitoring and censorship initiatives under the pretext of national security imperatives.

In sum, the diverse reactions from international governments in the wake of Snowden's revelations reflect the complex geopolitical dynamics and divergent national interests at stake. The fallout from these responses fundamentally reshaped the discourse surrounding surveillance governance and set the stage for a new era of global collaboration and contention in the realm of intelligence and privacy.

Changes in Global Surveillance Policies

In the wake of Edward Snowden's revelations, the leaking of classified information on global surveillance programs administered by the United States and its allies ignited a firestorm of controversy that reverberated around the world. The subsequent impact on global surveillance policies was profound, triggering a wave of scrutiny, debate, and reform. Governments across the globe were compelled to reevaluate their own surveillance practices, leading to a transformative shift in the landscape of international intelligence gathering. The disclosures prompted a reexamination of the balance between security imperatives and individual privacy rights. Countries previously considered to be close allies found themselves embroiled in diplomatic tension as speculation swirled about the extent of their involvement in mass surveillance. This forced governments to reassess their relationships and the level of trust among allies. As a result, an era of increased transparency in surveillance programs began to unfold, with several nations enacting legislative reforms to enhance oversight, accountability, and legal safeguards for citizens' privacy. Moreover, international cooperation on surveillance matters underwent significant recalibration, as countries sought to redefine the boundaries of permissible intelligence collection to align with ethical and legal standards. The revelations brought to the forefront the need for multilateral agreements and norms governing the conduct of intelligence operations, prompting intense discussions within global forums such as the United Nations and the European Union. A new era of transnational dialogue emerged, focusing on establishing principles for responsible surveillance and ensuring respect for human rights in the digital age. This period of introspection and adjustment shaped the evolution of surveillance policies worldwide, marking a turning point in the history of intelligence gathering and paving the way for a more transparent, accountable, and rights-respecting approach to global surveillance.

Impact on U.S. Foreign Relations

The disclosure of extensive surveillance activities by the National Security Agency (NSA) had a profound impact on U.S. foreign relations. It strained diplomatic ties, eroded trust, and generated deep-seated concern among allies and adversaries alike. The revelations brought to light the extent of U.S. intelligence gathering not only domestically but also internationally, sparking widespread outrage and apprehension.

In the aftermath of Edward Snowden's disclosures, numerous countries expressed strong condemnation of the U.S. government's surveillance practices. Traditional allies such as Germany, France, and Brazil voiced their dismay at the breach of privacy and the violation of their sovereignty. These revelations led to an urgent need for damage control, with diplomats facing the challenge of rebuilding trust and repairing fractured relationships.

Furthermore, the fallout from the leaks significantly affected intelligence-sharing agreements and cooperation between the U.S. and other nations. The exposure of clandestine surveillance programs strained vital channels of communication and cooperation in areas such as counterterrorism and cybersecurity. This upheaval underscored the critical importance of maintaining mutual trust and transparency in the realm of international intelligence sharing.

Moreover, the impact on U.S. foreign relations extended beyond immediate diplomatic repercussions. It influenced global perceptions of

American leadership and values, raising questions about the adherence to democratic principles and respect for individual privacy beyond U.S. borders. These concerns reverberated in multilateral forums and bilateral discussions, prompting reevaluations of the U.S.'s role in shaping global norms and standards for data privacy and security.

As a result of the seismic shift in international perception, the U.S. found itself compelled to address the implications of its surveillance activities on foreign policy initiatives. Efforts were made to assuage the anxieties of allies and reassure the international community of the U.S.'s commitment to respecting the privacy and sovereignty of other nations. Nevertheless, the ripple effects of the NSA revelations left an indelible mark on U.S. foreign relations, altering the geopolitical landscape and recalibrating the dynamics of international diplomacy.

Shifts in International Data Protection Laws

As the revelations of Edward Snowden sent shockwaves across the globe, it became evident that existing data protection laws were insufficient to address the implications of mass surveillance on a global scale. Governments and regulatory bodies worldwide were prompted to reevaluate and reform their data protection and privacy laws to safeguard citizens from potential infringements on their rights to privacy and personal autonomy.

In response to the revelations of widespread government surveillance, many countries undertook substantial amendments to their data protection legislation. The European Union, for instance, implemented the landmark General Data Protection Regulation (GDPR), which brought about radical changes in the way personal data is handled and protected. The GDPR not only strengthened individuals' control over their personal information but also imposed stringent requirements on organizations regarding data collection, storage, and processing, with severe penalties for non-compliance. Similarly, other regions and countries, including Brazil, Canada, and Australia, introduced or updated their data protection laws to address emerging challenges in the digital age.

Moreover, international efforts to harmonize data protection laws gained momentum as nations recognized the necessity for cohesive global standards. Collaborative initiatives and agreements aimed at fostering cross-border data protection, such as the APEC Privacy Framework and the Council of Europe's Convention 108, underscored the growing recognition of data privacy as a fundamental human right that transcends national boundaries. These developments reflected a collective commitment to fortifying individuals' privacy rights on an international scale while acknowledging the complex interconnectedness of modern data flows.

The shifts in international data protection laws also catalyzed changes in the business landscape, compelling organizations to adopt more transparent and ethical practices in handling personal data. The increased emphasis on accountability and transparency demanded a fundamental rethinking of data management strategies and incentivized companies to prioritize data protection as a core business imperative. Consequently, multinational corporations faced the imperative to align their operations with diverse legal frameworks, necessitating a concerted focus on compliance and governance across disparate jurisdictions.

Furthermore, the reformation of international data protection laws engendered a robust discourse on the delicate balance between security concerns and individual privacy rights. Debates surrounding government surveillance practices, lawful interception, and the permissible scope of data collection resounded across national legislatures and international forums, reflecting the intricate interplay between security imperatives and civil liberties. This deliberative process sought to reconcile divergent viewpoints and enunciate comprehensive frameworks that address security exigencies without encroaching upon fundamental rights.

In essence, the transformations in international data protection laws not only reframed the contours of privacy and consent but also delineated the collective resolve to establish a rights-based approach to data governance. These legislative developments engendered a paradigm shift in the conceptualization of privacy as a cornerstone of democratic societies, propelling the global community toward a future where data protection is enshrined as a fundamental human entitlement, underpinned by robust legal safeguards and ethical imperatives.

Public and Political Activation Worldwide

The revelations brought forward by Edward Snowden's leaks sparked significant public and political activation worldwide. From passionate individuals to influential organizations, a collective uproar against unchecked surveillance practices echoed across the globe. Citizens became acutely aware of the far-reaching implications of mass data collection, leading to widespread protests, petitions, and demands for greater transparency and accountability from governmental bodies. Simultaneously, political figures and policymakers found themselves engulfed in an intense discourse over the balance between national security imperatives and the fundamental right to privacy. This unprecedented surge of activism prompted a reevaluation of the norms governing intelligence-gathering methods and pushed governments to address public concerns earnestly. The impact was felt not only in established democracies but also in regions where freedom of expression and privacy rights faced perennial challenges. The development of grassroots movements advocating for digital rights and comprehensive reforms highlighted the global nature of the issue. Furthermore, citizens actively engaged with legislative processes, urging lawmakers to enact laws that safeguarded individual privacy without compromising on security interests. This newfound awareness and participation demonstrated the power of an informed and impassioned public in shaping the policies that governed their daily lives. International collaborative efforts and solidarity emerged as nations recognized common ground in addressing the complexities of surveillance and privacy in the digital age. The collective calls for change reverberated through international forums, influencing discussions on human rights, technological innovation, and governance on a global scale. As the landscape of surveillance and privacy continued to evolve, this era marked a pivotal juncture in the ongoing pursuit of a harmonious coexistence between security measures and civil liberties, fundamentally altering the dynamics of governance and societal expectations.

Technological Enhancements and Countermeasures

Technological advancements have played a pivotal role in shaping the response to the revelations made by Edward Snowden. Following the public disclosure of widespread surveillance activities, tech companies and innovators around the world embarked on an ambitious journey to fortify digital security and privacy. Companies engaged in diverse sectors, spanning from social media giants to telecommunication corporations, began prioritizing encryption, anonymity tools, and infrastructure hardening to protect user data and communications from unauthorized access.

In addition to bolstering defensive measures, the era post-Snowden witnessed a surge in the development and adoption of counter-surveillance technologies. An array of tools and services emerged to empower individuals and organizations with the means to safeguard their digital footprint. From secure messaging applications and anonymous browsing platforms to network-level encryption solutions, these innovations aimed to mitigate the risks posed by mass surveillance and government intrusion.

Moreover, the tech landscape witnessed a fervent pursuit of enhanced transparency and accountability mechanisms within digital platforms and services. With a heightened emphasis on empowering users to understand and control how their data is utilized, companies endeavored to introduce more accessible privacy settings, granular consent mechanisms, and comprehensive transparency reports. This shift towards increased transparency and user-centric control marked a defining transformation in the ethos of digital governance.

In essence, the technological response to the Snowden revelations transcended mere reactionary measures. It seeded a paradigm shift in the realm of digital security and privacy, fostering a culture of innovation that prioritizes empowerment, resilience, and ethical data practices. The subsequent chapters will delve into the enduring repercussions of these transformations, bearing witness to the intricate interplay between technology, policy, and societal perspectives on surveillance and privacy.

Economic Implications for Tech Companies

The revelations brought forward by Edward Snowden had substantial economic implications for technology companies, particularly those based in the United States. As the extent of government surveillance practices became public knowledge, various global stakeholders, including consumers and businesses, began to reevaluate their trust and reliance on American tech firms. This was primarily due to concerns about data privacy, security, and potential entanglement with state surveillance programs.

One immediate consequence was the erosion of international confidence in U.S.-based cloud service providers. Foreign governments and businesses started expressing apprehension about storing sensitive information with these companies, fearing that their data might be subject to clandestine access or monitoring by U.S. intelligence agencies. This raised significant challenges for tech giants such as Google, Microsoft, and Amazon as they sought to regain trust and reassure their global clientele.

Moreover, the economic impact extended to the realm of sales and market expansion. The tarnished reputations of these tech companies led to decreased sales in foreign markets, hindering their ability to expand globally. In response to this, many firms began to strategize alternative approaches, such as establishing data centers in other countries to mitigate concerns over U.S. jurisdiction and enable compliance with local data protection laws.

Additionally, the revelations prompted an upsurge in demand for secure communication and encryption technologies. Startups and established tech entities that specialized in encryption, secure messaging, and privacy-focused tools witnessed heightened interest and investment as businesses and individuals alike sought heightened protection from unwarranted surveillance. This trend fostered a shift in the technological landscape, spawning an array of innovative solutions geared towards safeguarding digital communications and securing data across various platforms.

Furthermore, in response to the shifting economic climate, companies also intensified their focus on transparency and privacy-centric features in their products and services. Enhanced privacy controls, encrypted messaging options, and robust security measures were integrated into offerings to assuage consumer concerns and align with evolving global attitudes towards data protection and privacy rights. Importantly, these shifts in product development and marketing strategies underscored the emerging emphasis on privacy as a competitive differentiator among tech companies striving to rebuild trust and maintain market relevance.

The economic consequences for tech companies following the Snowden disclosures thus epitomized a pivotal juncture in the interplay between digital surveillance, corporate trust, and global business dynamics. These implications continue to resonate within the tech industry, permeating strategic decision-making, product innovation, and competitive positioning in the ever-evolving landscape of digital commerce and technological advancement.

Global Discussions and Debates on Privacy vs. Security

The global impact of Edward Snowden's revelations stirred a heated debate regarding the delicate balance between privacy and security. Governments and policymakers worldwide faced mounting pressure to address concerns related to mass surveillance, collecting and storing . citizen data, and the protection of individual privacy rights. As the public became more aware of the extent of government surveillance and data collection, discussions on the boundaries between national security interests and personal privacy gained prominence. Countries around the world engaged in fervent debates, acknowledging the need for robust security measures while safeguarding citizens' fundamental rights to privacy.

The discourse surrounding privacy versus security extended beyond political circles, permeating various sectors of society, including the technological industry, legal fraternity, academia, and civil rights advocates. Technology giants strived to find a middle ground, grappling with the ethical implications of their role in data collection, storage, and sharing practices. Legal experts delved into complex constitutional and human rights issues, offering insights and opinions on striking an equilibrium between security imperatives and individual freedoms. Academia contributed rigorous analyses and research, enriching the discourse with empirical evidence and theoretical frameworks.

Civil liberties organizations and privacy advocates mobilized global attention toward the erosion of privacy rights in the digital age, spearheading movements for legislative changes and greater transparency in surveillance activities. These initiatives compelled governments to re-evaluate existing laws and regulations governing surveillance, resulting in substantive reforms aimed at preserving civil liberties while maintaining robust security protocols. The ongoing dialogue surrounding privacy and security also galvanized public engagement, sparking widespread activism and consciousness about digital rights and the implications of pervasive surveillance.

International forums and conferences became platforms for key stakeholders to converge, deliberating on the broader societal implications of unfettered surveillance practices and the necessity of bolstering security measures. Diverse perspectives and dissenting opinions coalesced, fueling conversations that transcended geopolitical boundaries. The global dialogue underscored the interconnectedness of privacy and security concerns, emphasizing the need for collaborative, multilateral approaches to address these complex challenges.

Amidst the multifaceted discussions, varying cultural and legal contexts across different nations gave rise to nuanced interpretations of privacy and security paradigms. Fostering mutual understanding and consensus-building emerged as imperative tenets in navigating the labyrinthine landscape of global privacy and security debates. As the discourse continued to evolve, the intricate interplay between individual rights, collective security, and technological advancements remained a focal point of global dialogue, encapsulating the enduring tensions and aspirations for a harmonious balance between privacy and security in the digital era.

Summary and Transition to Public Perception

The global impact of Edward Snowden's revelations on the far-reaching surveillance activities conducted by the U.S. National Security Agency has triggered an unprecedented global dialogue on the delicate balance between privacy and security. As governments, advocacy groups, and citizens around the world grapple with the implications of Snowden's disclosures, public perception has become a crucial aspect of the ongoing debate. The summary and transition to public perception serve as a pivotal point in understanding the enduring impact of Snowden's actions. From examining the shifting landscape of public opinion to delving into the ethical dilemmas associated with mass surveillance, this section aims to provide a comprehensive analysis of the complex interplay between individual privacy rights and national security considerations. In the aftermath of the disclosures, the spotlight turned towards how various stakeholders – from policymakers and technology companies to civil society organizations and everyday citizens – perceive the trade-offs between privacy and security in the digital age. The summary and transition to public perception will unveil the nuanced layers that underpin this consequential discourse. It will delineate the evolution of public sentiment, capture the divergent perspectives that have surfaced across diverse communities, and shed light on the factors that have shaped these varying perceptions. Moreover, this section will underscore the pivotal role of public perception in influencing policy decisions, motivating legislative reforms, and catalyzing technological innovations designed to safeguard individual privacy and civil liberties. By transitioning from the overarching global impact to public perception, this section will illustrate the profound implications of Snowden's actions on shaping the contemporary dialogue surrounding surveillance, privacy, and democratic principles. Throughout this exploration, readers will gain insights into the challenges and opportunities arising from the transformed public perception, laying the foundation for the subsequent chapters that delve deeper into the enduring ramifications and unresolved controversies stemming from the Snowden saga.

13

Public Perception: Hero, Traitor, and Somewhere in Between

The Complex Portrait of Edward Snowden

Edward Snowden's public image is a subject of intense debate and dissonance, embodying a multilayered enigma that elicits divergent perceptions. Revered by some as a courageous champion of civil liberties and democratic values, he remains reviled by others who label him a dangerous traitor and enemy of the state. This dichotomy has spawned an inherently complex and intricate portrayal of Snowden, with his actions sparking polarized views that have permeated through public consciousness. On one hand, supporters laud his decision to disclose classified information as an act of moral rectitude, positioning him as a valiant whistleblower unearthing government overreach and surveillance abuses. Conversely, detractors castigate his disclosures as jeopardizing national security and casting a shadow on the integrity of intelligence operations, framing him as a disloyal defector and transgressor of the law. The confounding juxtaposition of these contrasting perspectives creates an enigmatic persona, shaping an indeterminate legacy that continues to resonate within the global arena of privacy, security, and individual freedoms.

Public Opinion Polls: A Snapshot of Sentiments

Public opinion polls present a valuable lens through which we can gauge the diverse and often polarized sentiments that surround the controversial figure of Edward Snowden. These snapshots of public sentiment provide an insightful understanding of how individuals, communities, and nations view Snowden's actions and their underlying implications. With a complex mixture of admiration, suspicion, and dissent, these opinion polls demonstrate the nuanced and multifaceted nature of public perceptions.

The diversity of viewpoints depicted in these polls is striking. While some respondents laud Snowden as a courageous champion of civil liberties and transparency, others vilify him as a threat to national security and a traitor to his country. The sheer breadth of these contrasting perspectives underscores the intricate tapestry of sentiments that exist within society. Furthermore, regional variations in sentiment reveal that attitudes towards Snowden differ substantially across geographic boundaries and cultural contexts. These variations add layers of complexity to the analysis of public opinion and suggest that individual and collective values significantly influence perceptions.

The evolution of public sentiment over time is also a crucial aspect to consider. As new information emerges and societal attitudes shift, public opinion towards Snowden has exhibited dynamic fluctuations. Initial shock and skepticism have given way to a more nuanced evaluation of his motivations and actions. Furthermore, the impact of media coverage and geopolitical developments has exerted a profound influence on the trajectory of public opinion. These changing dynamics illuminate the transient nature of public sentiment and prompt reflection on the malleability of popular views.

Moreover, the methodology and framing of opinion polls themselves are subjects of substantial interest and scrutiny. It is paramount to acknowledge that the phrasing of questions, sampling methodologies, and context of surveys can significantly influence the outcomes of these polls. Critical examination of these factors not only enriches our understanding of public opinion but also underscores the intricate interplay between data collection and the formation of public sentiment.

In summary, public opinion polls serve as a critical instrument for apprehending the intricate and fluctuating sentiments surrounding Edward Snowden. By delving into these snapshots of public sentiment, we gain meaningful insights into the diverse array of perspectives, the evolution of public sentiment over time, and the impact of varied methodologies. Understanding these multifaceted sentiments is indispensable as we navigate the broader discourse on surveillance, personal freedoms, and ethical responsibilities in the digital age.

Media Portrayals: From Villain to Martyr

The media's representation of Edward Snowden has been a complex and ever-evolving narrative, oscillating between stark dichotomies of heroism and treason. Initially, following the monumental leaks, mainstream media often depicted Snowden as a traitor, emphasizing the potential damage his actions caused to national security. Media outlets, aligned with the government's stance, framed him as a defector who jeopardized the safety of the nation and therefore as a villainous figure. However, as more information surfaced and public discourse developed, alternative narratives emerged. Certain journalists and news platforms began to illustrate Snowden as a brave whistleblower, shedding light on unlawful government surveillance and championing civil liberties. This portrayal positioned him as a martyr for human rights, invoking historical archetypes of individuals who sacrifice personal comfort for the greater good. The media landscape became a battleground where contrasting perspectives clashed, and Snowden's image shifted dynamically. This transformation reflected the broader societal struggle to categorize a man whose actions defied simplistic classification. Moreover, profound debates unfolded within media circles, amplifying the contested portrayal of this enigmatic figure. It is crucial to recognize how the media's portrayal of Edward Snowden has significantly influenced public perception, contributing to the enduring polarization of sentiments surrounding his disclosures and subsequent exile.

Government Responses and Rhetoric Against Snowden

Edward Snowden's actions sent shockwaves through the halls of power, prompting an array of strong and often heated responses from governments around the world. The United States government, in particular, vehemently condemned his actions, labeling him a traitor and emphasizing the potential harm caused by the disclosure of classified information. High-ranking officials within the U.S. government portrayed Snowden as a threat to national security and sought to discredit his motivations, painting him as a disgruntled employee who had put lives at risk. This rhetoric against Snowden was echoed by other key allies and international bodies, reflecting the extent to which his actions disrupted established norms of secrecy and surveillance. Beyond the immediate denunciations, it sparked debates about the limits of governmental authority and the rights of individuals to challenge state power in the name of transparency and public interest. Proposals for legal action against Snowden also emerged, which further polarized public opinion over the legitimacy of his actions. Governments across the globe framed their responses within the context of national security imperatives, portraying the disclosure of sensitive information as a breach of trust with far-reaching implications. The diplomatic fallout from Snowden's disclosures strained relations between the United States and several nations, establishing a backdrop of heightened geopolitical tensions and legal ramifications. This section explores the multifaceted landscape of governmental reactions to Edward Snowden's revelations, shedding light on the intricate interplay between state power, individual agency, and the shifting dynamics of global politics in the digital age.

Support from Civil Rights Groups

Support from civil rights groups has been a significant aspect in the ongoing debate surrounding Edward Snowden. Various organizations dedicated to protecting civil liberties and individual privacy rights have emerged as vocal advocates for Snowden's actions. These groups argue that Snowden's disclosures have shed light on government overreach and surveillance abuses, sparking crucial discussions about the balance between national security and personal freedoms. The American Civil Liberties Union (ACLU) has been at the forefront, emphasizing the importance of holding government agencies accountable for their surveillance practices. Through legal advocacy and public campaigns, the ACLU has sought to challenge the legality and scope of the surveillance programs brought to light by Snowden. Similarly, the Electronic Frontier Foundation (EFF) has pursued litigation and policy initiatives aimed at safeguarding digital privacy and limiting mass surveillance. These organizations, alongside others such as Amnesty International and Human Rights Watch, have rallied behind Snowden, framing his actions as bold efforts to protect fundamental human rights. They have underscored the need for robust whistleblower protections and transparency in government surveillance programs. Moreover, civil rights groups have amplified the conversation on the implications of mass surveillance on marginalized communities, highlighting how these practices disproportionately impact minority groups and infringe upon their rights. By aligning with Snowden's cause, these organizations have broadened the discourse on surveillance, linking it to broader social justice and equity concerns. Their support has shaped public discourse, challenging the portrayal of Snowden as solely a threat to national security and casting him instead as a catalyst for critical reform. As a result, the involvement of civil rights groups has significantly contributed to reframing the narrative around Snowden, elevating the discussion beyond individual culpability to encompass systemic issues of privacy, accountability, and human rights.

Social Media Influence on Perception

The rise of social media has revolutionized the way information is disseminated and received. In the case of Edward Snowden, social media platforms have played a crucial role in shaping public perception of his actions and motivations. The immediacy and interconnectedness afforded by social media have allowed for the rapid spread of diverse opinions, news articles, and personal testimonies relating to Snowden and the issues he brought to light. This section aims to examine the influence of social media on the public's understanding of Edward Snowden, highlighting both the positive and negative aspects of this impact.

One of the key ways in which social media has influenced public perception is through the amplification of voices from various stances. Supporters of Snowden have utilized platforms such as Twitter, Facebook, and Reddit to share sympathetic narratives, engage in advocacy, and organize events or petitions in his defense. Simultaneously, critics and detractors have leveraged these same platforms to cast doubt on Snowden's character, criticize his disclosure of classified information, and perpetuate the debate around the consequences of his actions. The resulting echo chamber effect can entrench existing opinions and polarize the discourse, making it challenging for individuals to access balanced perspectives.

Moreover, the proliferation of misinformation and conspiracy theories on social media has further complicated the public's perception of Edward Snowden. False narratives and sensationalized accounts have circulated widely, contributing to a distorted and fragmented understanding of his motives and the implications of his revelations. These distortions have deepened the divide between those who consider Snowden a hero and those who view him as a traitor, impeding constructive dialogue about the broader issues of surveillance and privacy.

In contrast, social media has also facilitated valuable conversations and critical analysis that have broadened public understanding of Snowden's disclosures and their implications. Independent journalists, activists, and academics have used social media platforms to provide nuanced perspectives, investigate legal and ethical dimensions, and engage audiences in thoughtful debates. Furthermore, the direct engagement of Edward Snowden himself on social media has offered a unique window into his thoughts, enabling the public to gain insight into his motivations and values directly from the source.

Overall, the influence of social media on public perception of Edward Snowden is multi-faceted, encompassing both constructive and detrimental effects. While it has empowered diverse voices and democratized public discourse, it has also catalyzed polarization and exacerbated misinformation. Understanding and navigating these dynamics is essential for comprehensively appreciating the complex and often divergent perceptions surrounding one of the most polarizing figures in contemporary history.

Cultural Impact and Artistic Representations

The cultural impact of Edward Snowden's actions has been profound, permeating various forms of artistic expression that seek to encapsulate the complex facets of his narrative. From literature to film, music, and visual arts, Snowden's story has resonated with creators and audiences alike, sparking a wave of productions that delve into themes of government surveillance, individual liberties, and the ethical dimensions of whistleblowing. In literature, numerous authors have drawn inspiration from Snowden's disclosures, weaving them into narratives that explore the tension between state power and personal freedom. These works serve as a testament to the lasting impression of Snowden's revelations on contemporary storytelling. Additionally, cinema has embraced Snowden's saga, with several documentaries and feature films providing cinematic interpretations of his journey, inviting viewers to contemplate the consequences of unchecked surveillance and the sacrifices made in the pursuit of truth. Music, too, has not been immune to the influence of Snowden's legacy, as artists across genres have incorporated his experiences and ideals into their lyrics, highlighting the enduring relevance of his message in the realm of popular culture. Visual arts have also played a role in capturing the essence of Snowden's struggle, with paintings, photographs, and other visual media offering unique perspectives on the moral dilemmas inherent in modern-day surveillance practices. These artistic representations serve as crucial platforms for fostering dialogue and introspection, prompting audiences to consider the societal implications of mass data collection and the principles that underpin individual agency. By examining the plethora of artistic responses to Snowden's narrative, it becomes evident that his impact extends far beyond the realms of politics and law, permeating the creative landscape in a manner that attests to the enduring significance of his actions. As the cultural resonance of Snowden's story continues to unfold, it signals the enduring power of art to provoke critical examination of the world we inhabit, offering new vantage points from which to contemplate the intersection of authority, privacy, and the human experience.

Comparative Perspectives: Snowden vs. Other Whistleblowers

The comparison between Edward Snowden and other whistleblowers is a nuanced exploration of their respective actions, impact, and public reception. While Snowden's revelations exposed the extent of global surveillance programs, it is essential to examine how his case differs from those of other prominent whistleblowers throughout history. One such figure is Daniel Ellsberg, renowned for leaking the Pentagon Papers, which detailed the United States' covert involvement in Vietnam. Both Snowden and Ellsberg faced accusations of treason, yet they were also lauded by supporters as courageous truth-tellers. This parallel invites an analysis of the evolving societal attitudes towards whistleblowers and the shifting dynamics of state secrecy. Additionally, Chelsea Manning's disclosure of classified military documents highlighted the complexities of information dissemination and provoked debates on the ethics of leaking sensitive materials. Contrasting the circumstances and consequences of Manning's and Snowden's actions elucidates the multifaceted nature of whistleblowing. Moreover, the comparison extends to international whistleblowers, such as Julian Assange, whose organization WikiLeaks facilitated the publication of confidential documents. Assessing the global implications of Assange's activities alongside Snowden's revelations broadens the scope of understanding the impact of whistleblowers beyond national borders. Furthermore, historical figures like W. Mark Felt, also known as 'Deep Throat' during the Watergate scandal, serve as a reference point in examining the intersection of whistleblowing, journalism, and institutional accountability. Drawing parallels between Felt's covert disclosures and Snowden's deliberate public exposure navigates the intricate web of motivations and outcomes inherent in whistleblowing acts. The comparative study of Snowden and other whistleblowers unveils a tapestry of ethical considerations, legal frameworks, and public narratives that shape the broader discourse on government transparency, individual conscience, and the balance of power in democratic societies.

Shifts in Public Opinion Over Time

Public opinion regarding Edward Snowden has experienced significant shifts over time, reflecting the evolving global discourse on government surveillance, privacy rights, and whistleblowing. Initially, when Snowden's revelations first emerged, public sentiment was divided, with many viewing him as a traitor who endangered national security by disclosing classified information. Government officials and intelligence agencies also portrayed him as a reckless individual who had jeopardized the safety of citizens.

However, as more details of the extensive surveillance programs conducted by government entities came to light, there was a marked change in public perception. Many individuals began to recognize Snowden as a courageous whistleblower who had shed light on unprecedented intrusions into personal privacy and civil liberties. This shift was fueled by growing concerns about the far-reaching implications of mass surveillance and the erosion of fundamental rights in the digital age.

Over time, public support for Snowden intensified as his disclosures spurred widespread debates on the ethical boundaries of governmental surveillance and the need for transparency and accountability. Advocates of free speech and privacy rights championed Snowden as a defender of democratic values, while critics raised questions about the government's overreach and the scope of its surveillance capabilities.

As discussions on these issues unfolded in the public sphere, the portrayal of Snowden in popular culture and media narratives continued to evolve. His story became the subject of books, documentaries, and films, shaping his image as a polarizing figure whose actions prompted critical reflections on power, authority, and the role of dissent in modern society.

Furthermore, the impact of social media in amplifying diverse viewpoints and fostering grassroots movements contributed to the diversification of public opinion regarding Snowden. Digital platforms provided a space for dialogue and mobilization, enabling individuals from different backgrounds to voice their perspectives and engage in discourses that questioned established narratives.

In summary, the evolution of public opinion on Edward Snowden reflects the dynamic interplay between political, legal, social, and cultural dynamics. The ongoing debate surrounding his actions underscores the complexities of modern governance and the enduring struggle to reconcile security imperatives with individual liberties and democratic values. These shifts in public sentiment serve as a poignant backdrop to the broader ethical considerations surrounding surveillance and the responsible exercise of power.

Summary and Segue into the Ethics of Surveillance

The shifts in public opinion over time regarding Edward Snowden have shed light on the complexity of his portrayal in the eyes of the public. From the initial shockwaves of his revelations to the ongoing debates about his actions, Snowden remains a polarizing figure. As the discourse surrounding Snowden continues to evolve, it becomes increasingly evident that his legacy extends far beyond the realms of heroism or treachery.

This nuanced understanding sets the stage for a deeper examination of the underlying ethical considerations that underpin Snowden's whistleblowing efforts. It serves as a bridge between the perceptions of an individual and the broader implications for society. By delving into the ethics of surveillance, we are compelled to address fundamental questions about privacy, government accountability, and the balance between national security and individual freedoms.

At the heart of this transition is the realization that the narrative surrounding Edward Snowden cannot be fully comprehended without grappling with the broader ethical landscape of modern surveillance practices. The intertwining of personal perceptions and societal implications emphasizes the need for a multidimensional approach, one that transcends simplistic labels of hero or traitor.

As we navigate this segue, it becomes imperative to confront the moral significance of surveillance in the digital age. This entails scrutinizing the mechanisms through which personal data is collected, analyzed, and utilized by governmental entities and private corporations. The juxtaposition of competing interests – security imperatives versus individual rights – fosters a crucial dialogue concerning the boundaries of acceptable conduct in the name of national security.

Furthermore, the ethical dimensions extend beyond the mere collection of information; they encompass the dissemination, storage, and potential misuse of data. This speaks to the intricate web of power dynamics and the imperative to uphold transparency and oversight in surveillance practices. Through this lens, Snowden's actions serve as a catalyst for profound introspection, prompting society to grapple with the implications of an increasingly interconnected and monitored world.

By setting the stage for an exploration of these multifaceted ethical considerations, this transition from public perception to the ethics of surveillance propels the narrative forward, inviting readers to discern the complexities that underlie the global debate sparked by Edward Snowden's courageous actions.

14

The Ethics of Surveillance

In the modern age of technological advancement, the debate surrounding the ethics of surveillance has reached a critical juncture. As society grapples with the implications of pervasive surveillance on individual privacy and civil liberties, it becomes imperative to critically examine the ethical considerations inherent in the practice of surveillance.

Surveillance, in its various forms, presents a complex ethical landscape. On one hand, proponents argue that surveillance measures are essential for maintaining public safety and security. They assert that surveillance technologies serve as a deterrent to criminal activities and act as a safeguard against potential threats to national and global security. Proponents also contend that surveillance can aid in the prevention, investigation, and prosecution of crimes, thereby contributing to the broader goal of societal well-being.

Conversely, opponents of widespread surveillance emphasize the infringements upon personal privacy and individual freedoms that can result from unchecked surveillance practices. They argue that unchecked surveillance can lead to a pervasive culture of suspicion and erode trust within communities. Moreover, opponents stress the potential for abuse of surveillance powers by both state and non-state actors, leading to the manipulation and exploitation of personal information for nefarious purposes.

Ethical considerations also extend to the methods of surveillance employed. The utilization of advanced technologies, such as facial recognition, biometric data collection, and mass data interception, raises ethical questions pertaining to potential misuse and the ever-present risk of privacy breaches. The ethical implications of data retention, storage, and accessibility further compound these concerns, as the potential for unauthorized access and misuse of personal information remains a prevalent issue.

Moreover, the rapid evolution of surveillance technologies, particularly in the realm of artificial intelligence and machine learning, raises pressing ethical questions about the potential for algorithmic biases and discrimination. The reliance on automated decision-making processes in surveillance systems introduces ethical complexities regarding transparency, accountability, and fairness, particularly when it comes to the identification and tracking of individuals.

The ethical implications of surveillance are not confined solely to actions of governmental bodies and law enforcement agencies. Private sector involvement in surveillance activities, particularly in the realm of data collection and analysis, raises pertinent ethical questions regarding corporate responsibility, consumer rights, and the commodification of personal information. The monetization of surveillance data and the potential for its exploitation in targeted advertising, behavioral manipulation, and market segmentation further complicates the ethical landscape.

The intertwining of surveillance and power dynamics deserves deep consideration. The potential for surveillance to be used as a tool for social control and the stifling of dissent brings to light profound ethical dilemmas. The specter of mass surveillance being exploited to suppress political opposition or to target marginalized communities underscores the far-reaching impact of surveillance activities on the fabric of society, raising profound ethical questions about the distribution and exercise of power in a democratic society.

Furthermore, the ethical dimensions of surveillance extend to global implications, as international surveillance practices raise questions about transnational privacy norms, data sharing, and the sovereignty of nations in relation to surveillance activities carried out beyond their borders. The potential for surveillance to become a tool of geopolitical influence, espionage, and cyberwarfare underscores the ethical complexity entwined with modern surveillance practices and prompts the need for international cooperation and ethical guidelines to mitigate potential abuse and violations of human rights.

In light of these ethical complexities, a robust framework for surveillance ethics becomes imperative. This framework must transcend narrow interests and instead prioritize the preservation of individual liberties and human rights while acknowledging the necessity of security measures. It is incumbent upon society, policymakers, and technological innovators to navigate this ethical minefield with prudence, mindfulness, and a commitment to upholding the fundamental rights of individuals.

The ongoing discourse on the ethics of surveillance serves as a testament to the pivotal intersection of technology, governance, and individual rights. As the contours of surveillance continue to evolve, the ethical considerations surrounding its practice remain a paramount concern, demanding the conscientious deliberation and ethical fortitude of all stakeholders involved. As we continue to grapple with these complex and profound ethical challenges, it is essential to seek a harmonious balance between security imperatives and the protection of individual rights, ensuring that surveillance remains within ethical boundaries that honor the dignity and autonomy of every person.

15

The Ripple Effects: Changes in Policy and Technology

Post-Snowden Reforms

In the wake of the unprecedented disclosures made by Edward Snowden, the United States was compelled to initiate significant reforms and policy changes in response to the revelations of extensive surveillance programs. The public outcry and global repercussions prompted immediate action on various legislative fronts. The initial wave of post-Snowden reforms sought to reassure citizens and allies while addressing concerns around civil liberties, privacy rights, and governmental overreach. This section delves into the multifaceted landscape of legislative responses in the United States, tracing the trajectory of this pivotal period in the nation's history. At the forefront were endeavors to restore public trust and redefine the boundaries of permissible surveillance activities. These efforts entailed bipartisan initiatives aimed at fortifying oversight mechanisms, enhancing transparency, and curbing unchecked data collection practices. Both the executive and legislative branches were instrumental in formulating and enacting measures designed to recalibrate the balance between national security imperatives and individual privacy safeguards. The shift in discourse surrounding surveillance and intelligence operations catalyzed comprehensive reviews of existing legal frameworks, compelling lawmakers to confront the evolving complexities of modern technology and communications. The introduction of post-Snowden reforms set the stage for in-depth deliberations on the scope and limitations of surveillance authorities vested in government agencies. Concurrently, the focus on reinforcing constitutional safeguards and reinforcing the checks and balances within the intelligence community fueled spirited debates that reverberated across political arenas and public forums. This chapter not only examines the immediate aftermath of Snowden's disclosures but also dissects the nuanced dynamics underlying the formulation and implementation of reforms that indelibly reshaped the landscape of national security and privacy governance.

Legislative Responses in the United States

In the wake of Edward Snowden's revelations about the extent of government surveillance, the United States experienced a significant shift in legislative attitudes towards national security and citizens' rights to privacy. The release of classified information by Snowden sparked intense debate on the balance between security measures and the protection of civil liberties. As a response, several key pieces of legislation and executive actions were introduced to address the concerns raised by the public and various stakeholders. One of the most notable developments was the passage of the USA Freedom Act in 2015, which marked a decisive turning point in the government's approach to intelligence gathering and mass data collection.

The USA Freedom Act brought about substantial changes to the legal framework governing surveillance activities, particularly with regard to the bulk collection of telecommunication metadata. Under this legislation, the National Security Agency (NSA) underwent a transformation in its practices, as provisions were made to curb the agency's ability to indiscriminately gather and store vast amounts of communication data. Moreover, the Act introduced heightened transparency and accountability requirements for the government's surveillance programs, compelling authorities to report on the scope and nature of their data collection efforts to oversight bodies and the public.

In addition to statutory reforms, there were pivotal judicial decisions that reshaped the landscape of surveillance law in the United States. Notably, the high-profile case of ACLU v. Clapper brought the legality of the NSA's bulk collection program into sharp focus, leading to a landmark ruling by the Second Circuit Court of Appeals that declared the program illegal under the Patriot Act. This decision reverberated throughout the legal sphere and compelled lawmakers to reevaluate the permissible scope of surveillance activities and the adequacy of existing legal safeguards.

Furthermore, the evolving discourse on digital privacy and the need for enhanced safeguards led to executive actions from the highest echelons of government. The administration of President Barack Obama initiated measures to bolster the protection of individual privacy rights, and ushered in a new era of collaboration between technology companies and government agencies to ensure responsible data handling practices and uphold the principles of privacy by design.

The collective impact of these legislative and regulatory initiatives was wide-ranging, fostering a climate of renewed scrutiny and accountability within the nation's intelligence apparatus. The interplay between national security imperatives and civil liberties reached a critical juncture, and the resulting reforms underscored the enduring influence of Edward Snowden's disclosures on the trajectory of surveillance policy in the United States.

Changes in EU Data Protection Laws

The revelations brought forth by Edward Snowden's unprecedented disclosures of widespread surveillance practices not only sparked a global outcry but also triggered significant reforms in data protection laws and regulations around the world. In the European Union (EU), the impact was particularly profound, leading to an overhaul of existing data protection frameworks. One of the most notable developments was the introduction of the General Data Protection Regulation (GDPR) in 2018, which replaced the outdated Data Protection Directive of 1995. The GDPR aimed to strengthen data protection for individuals within the EU and the European Economic Area, while also addressing the export of personal data outside the region. Its provisions included stricter requirements for obtaining consent, enhanced rights for data subjects, and increased accountability for organizations handling personal data. Moreover, the GDPR introduced hefty penalties for non-compliance, underlining the gravity with which data privacy is now regarded within the EU. The regulation has had far-reaching implications on businesses and institutions operating in or dealing with EU citizens' data, prompting them to implement extensive measures to ensure compliance. As such, the GDPR exemplifies how Snowden's disclosures catalyzed a fundamental shift in the legal landscape surrounding data protection, redefining the expectations and standards for privacy across the EU. Additionally, the Snowden revelations have influenced ongoing discussions regarding transatlantic data transfers and the adequacy of data protection safeguards in the context of EU-US relations. The European Court of Justice's landmark decision in the Schrems II case, which struck down the EU-US Privacy Shield, further underscored the impact of Snowden's actions on shaping the legal framework for international data flows. Consequently, the changes in EU data protection laws as a response to the Snowden disclosures continue to reverberate, illustrating the enduring influence of this pivotal moment in contemporary history on the evolution of privacy rights and legislation.

Technological Innovations for Privacy Enhancement

Technological advancements have played a crucial role in reshaping the landscape of privacy and data protection in the wake of Edward Snowden's revelations. In the aftermath of widespread surveillance disclosures, there has been a surge in innovative technologies aimed at enhancing personal privacy and safeguarding sensitive information from unauthorized access. These innovations encompass a diverse array of tools, ranging from secure communication platforms to advanced encryption protocols and anonymizing networks.

One key area of innovation is the development of secure messaging apps and communication platforms that prioritize end-to-end encryption, effectively preventing third-party interception and scrutiny. By implementing robust encryption methodologies, these technologies empower individuals and organizations to communicate securely without the fear of surveillance or unwanted eavesdropping. Furthermore, these solutions often incorporate features such as self-destructing messages and anonymity controls, granting users greater control over their digital interactions and data sharing practices.

In addition to secure communication tools, the realm of privacy-enhancing technologies also encompasses sophisticated encryption protocols designed to protect data at rest and in transit. From advanced encryption algorithms to decentralized storage mechanisms, these solutions aim to fortify the security of sensitive information against potential breaches and unauthorized access. The widespread adoption of robust encryption not only bolsters individual privacy but also strengthens the overall resilience of digital infrastructure and data protection frameworks.

Furthermore, the emergence of anonymizing networks and privacy-focused browsing technologies has provided individuals with enhanced capabilities to shield their online activities and browsing habits from prying eyes. Anonymity networks, such as Tor (The Onion Router), route internet traffic through a series of encrypted relays, obscuring the origin and destination of data transmissions. This enables users to mitigate tracking attempts and browse the internet with a heightened degree of privacy and anonymity, reducing the risk of surveillance and behavioral profiling.

Moreover, technological advancements have spurred the proliferation of privacy-preserving tools and services tailored to mitigate the pervasive tracking and data collection practices employed by online entities. From ad-blocking extensions and anti-tracking mechanisms to browser privacy enhancements, these innovations offer users the means to assert greater control over their digital footprint and limit the dissemination of personal information to advertisers and data brokers.

In summation, the post-Snowden era has witnessed a surge in technological innovations dedicated to augmenting privacy protections and empowering individuals to navigate the digital realm with heightened security and confidentiality. These advancements signify a paradigm shift towards prioritizing privacy considerations in the design and deployment of digital technologies, ultimately fostering a more resilient and privacy-centric digital ecosystem.

Corporate Policy Overhauls and User Data

In the wake of Edward Snowden's revelations, corporations globally found themselves at a crossroads, forced to reassess their policies regarding user data and privacy. As public skepticism around data security heightened, companies had to pivot swiftly to rebuild trust and safeguard the personal information of their users. This monumental shift in approach resulted in comprehensive policy overhauls across sectors, impacting both technology giants and smaller entities.

One of the most notable changes stemmed from the growing acknowledgment of the responsibility that corporations held in protecting user data. Consequently, new protocols were implemented to ensure that user privacy was prioritized in product development and data handling. This entailed scrutinizing data collection practices, enhancing encryption measures, and providing users with greater control over their personal information. Moreover, transparency became a pivotal component of these overhauls, leading to the creation of clear and concise privacy policies intended to inform users about how their data was being utilized and secured.

Furthermore, the landscape of digital advertising underwent a significant transformation. Companies that relied on targeted advertising and user data for revenue faced mounting pressure to procure data ethically and solicit consent in a more transparent manner. As a result, there was a surge in the development of privacy-focused advertising solutions, assuring users that their data would not be exploited for commercial gain without their explicit permission.

Another marked change involved the internal restructuring of corporate teams dedicated to data privacy and security. Staffing increases in these departments became commonplace as companies sought to bolster their expertise and vigilance in safeguarding user data. From hiring chief privacy officers to establishing dedicated cross-functional privacy task forces, organizations made concerted efforts to fortify their capabilities in the face of evolving privacy concerns. These initiatives were further augmented by investments in employee training programs, ensuring that all staff members remained abreast of emerging best practices in data protection and privacy compliance.

The overarching impact of these corporate policy overhauls was a paradigm shift in the way user data was viewed and handled. By placing privacy at the forefront of their operations, corporations not only mitigated the risk of data breaches and regulatory penalties but also fostered an environment of trust and loyalty among their user base. Although these reforms posed initial challenges, they ultimately laid the foundation for a more ethical and conscientious approach to user data, aligning with the evolving expectations of a privacy-conscious society.

Impact on International Data Sharing Agreements

In the wake of Edward Snowden's revelations, international data sharing agreements underwent a seismic transformation. Numerous countries and multinational organizations were forced to reevaluate their existing arrangements for exchanging sensitive information. The disclosures about pervasive surveillance activities sparked widespread concern about the integrity and privacy of shared data. Governments realized that their citizens' information was potentially being accessed without consent or oversight, leading to heightened scrutiny of long-standing data sharing accords.

The fallout from Snowden's disclosures led to a cascade of reassessments and renegotiations of international data sharing agreements. Many governments faced pressure from their constituents and foreign partners to enhance transparency, accountability, and privacy protections within these arrangements. As a result, several high-level summits and diplomatic discussions took place to construct new frameworks that addressed the implications of mass surveillance on cross-border data sharing.

In response to the public outcry and diplomatic pressures, several nations engaged in bilateral and multilateral negotiations to amend or establish new international data sharing protocols. These revised agreements aimed to incorporate stricter safeguards against unwarranted access and misuse of exchanged information. Additionally, they sought to address concerns related to the potential exploitation of shared data for covert surveillance purposes.

Parties involved in such agreements faced the challenge of balancing national security imperatives with respect for individual privacy and civil liberties. This delicate balance necessitated thorough deliberations to redefine the scope and limitations of permissible data access in a globally connected yet privacy-conscious environment. Consequently, the landscape of international data sharing agreements witnessed a pronounced shift towards principles rooted in transparency, proportionality, and respect for user privacy.

The impact of these revamped data sharing accords rippled through various sectors, influencing cross-border commerce, law enforcement cooperation, and intelligence sharing initiatives. Notably, organizations and regulatory bodies grappled with aligning their practices with the evolving standards outlined in these revised agreements, fostering a climate of adaptability and adherence to heightened data protection norms.

Moreover, these developments spurred collaborative efforts to harmonize divergent data protection laws across jurisdictions. The emergence of mutual recognition frameworks and interoperability standards aimed to facilitate seamless data exchange while upholding robust privacy safeguards irrespective of geographic boundaries.

In essence, the revelations by Edward Snowden reverberated throughout the international community, instigating an era of reformation in data sharing practices. The resulting changes galvanized a collective commitment to fortify data sharing agreements with provisions that safeguard individual privacy rights and uphold ethical standards in an increasingly interconnected world.

Adjustments in Surveillance Practices by Governments

Governments across the globe have been compelled to reevaluate and modify their surveillance practices in the wake of the revelations brought forth by Edward Snowden. The exposure of widespread mass surveillance programs, including bulk data collection and indiscriminate monitoring, not only raised serious ethical and legal concerns but also triggered public outcry and demands for greater transparency and accountability. As a result, numerous governments have faced mounting pressure to justify their surveillance activities and enforce stricter oversight mechanisms.

In response to this heightened scrutiny, several nations have initiated reforms aimed at striking a balance between national security imperatives and individual privacy rights. Some have introduced or revised legislation to curtail unchecked government surveillance, imposing greater constraints on the scope and duration of data collection, mandating judicial approval for surveillance warrants, and enhancing mechanisms for independent oversight. These efforts signify an acknowledgment of the need to safeguard civil liberties while ensuring the effectiveness of intelligence-gathering operations.

Moreover, there has been a notable shift towards promoting transparency within governmental agencies involved in surveillance. Several countries have implemented measures to enhance public disclosure of surveillance practices, providing detailed reports on the nature and extent of data collection, as well as the mechanisms employed to minimize the impact on privacy. Additionally, efforts have been made to foster dialogue with privacy advocates, technology companies, and other stakeholders to garner diverse perspectives and input regarding the development of surveillance policies.

The paradigm shift induced by Snowden's disclosures has also prompted the exploration of alternative surveillance methodologies that prioritize targeted, intelligence-driven approaches over pervasive, dragnet surveillance. This has led to investments in sophisticated technological tools and analytical capabilities, enabling authorities to focus on specific threats while minimizing the intrusion into lawful activities of individuals. Such initiatives underscore a concerted effort to recalibrate surveillance strategies to align with principles of proportionality, necessity, and respect for privacy and human rights.

Furthermore, the global interconnectedness of modern communication networks has necessitated collaborative efforts among nations to harmonize surveillance practices in line with international norms and agreements. This has entailed exchanges of best practices, standardization of data protection protocols, and alignment with overarching human rights frameworks. By adopting a more cooperative approach, governments seek to ensure consistent standards while addressing transnational challenges posed by evolving technologies and cross-border information flows.

In conclusion, the aftermath of the Snowden disclosures has catalyzed a fundamental reassessment of surveillance practices by governments worldwide. This reevaluation has engendered a wave of reforms aimed at promoting accountability, transparency, and the responsible use of surveillance capabilities to uphold both national security imperatives and individual privacy rights. The enduring impact of these adjustments resonates in the ongoing discourse surrounding the delicate balance between security and privacy in an increasingly complex and interconnected digital landscape.

Influence on Cryptography and Encryption Techniques

The revelation of mass surveillance by government agencies, as exposed by Snowden, has had a profound impact on the field of cryptography and encryption techniques. It sparked a heightened focus on privacy and data security, leading to significant developments in the realm of digital protection. One notable consequence was the impetus for companies and organizations to bolster their efforts in creating more robust encryption methods to safeguard sensitive information from prying eyes. The Snowden disclosures underscored the critical need for stronger encryption across various communication platforms and data storage systems.

This heightened awareness of the vulnerabilities inherent in existing encryption protocols prompted a surge in research and development aimed at enhancing cryptographic algorithms and technologies. The result has been the emergence of advanced encryption standards that have empowered individuals and entities to protect their communications and data more effectively. Moreover, the Snowden revelations galvanized a renewed interest in end-to-end encryption, prompting many tech companies to integrate this feature into their products as a means of fortifying user privacy.

Furthermore, the public's growing concern over privacy infringements spurred an increased emphasis on user-friendly encryption tools and applications. Innovations in this space sought to democratize access to robust encryption, making it more accessible and comprehensible to the general populace. This shift has not only augmented individual privacy protections but also instilled a deeper understanding of encryption technologies among the wider public.

In the wake of these seismic shifts, the landscape of international data security protocols and regulations has experienced notable transformations.

Public Awareness and Advocacy Movements

In the wake of Edward Snowden's revelations about mass

surveillance, a groundswell of public awareness and advocacy movements emerged globally. These movements, which gained momentum in various parts of the world, sought to raise awareness about privacy rights, government overreach, and the implications of unchecked surveillance. Citizens, civil liberties organizations, and privacy advocates formed coalitions, organized protests, and utilized social media platforms to disseminate information and stimulate conversations about the delicate balance between national security and individual privacy.

In the United States, the disclosure of extensive government surveillance programs catalyzed the formation of grassroots networks focused on digital rights and privacy. Organizations such as the Electronic Frontier Foundation (EFF), American Civil Liberties Union (ACLU), and Fight for the Future played pivotal roles in mobilizing public engagement, engaging policymakers, and spearheading legal challenges aimed at protecting civil liberties in the digital age.

Beyond the borders of the U.S., the global impact of Snowden's disclosures reverberated profoundly. In Europe, Snowden's revelations prompted heightened scrutiny of intelligence practices, spurring efforts to strengthen data protection laws and enhance transparency measures. The emergence of campaigns like 'Reset the Net' and 'The Day We Fight Back' underscored an international coalition advocating for privacy-centered technological solutions and legislative reforms to safeguard personal data from unwarranted surveillance.

Moreover, Snowden's actions ignited a broader dialogue on the ethical responsibilities of technology companies and internet service providers. Industry giants faced mounting pressure from consumers and advocacy groups to bolster data encryption, adopt robust privacy policies, and resist government requests for access to user information. Consequently, this period witnessed a paradigm shift as tech companies reevaluated their role in protecting user privacy and actively participated in discussions regarding government surveillance reform.

The enduring legacy of public awareness and advocacy movements following Snowden's disclosures extends to contemporary debates surrounding surveillance, individual liberty, and the evolving landscape of digital privacy. While these movements engendered critical legislative reforms and incited discourse, they also underscore the enduring significance of citizen engagement in shaping policies that safeguard fundamental rights in an increasingly interconnected world.

Conclusion: Assessing the Long-Term Effects

The long-term consequences of Edward Snowden's revelations have undeniably reshaped the landscape of surveillance, privacy, and governance. As we've traversed the aftermath of Snowden's disclosures, it becomes paramount to evaluate the lasting impact on societal, political, and technological realms.

At the forefront, the heightened public awareness triggered by Snowden's actions led to an upsurge in advocacy movements championing digital rights and privacy. The dissemination of knowledge about government surveillance programs catalyzed an awakening, fueling a global demand for transparency and accountability in data collection practices. Consequently, this surge in public vigilance galvanized a wave of grassroots and legislative initiatives designed to fortify privacy protections and civil liberties on both national and international scales.

One of the most profound shifts has been observed in the realm of policy-making. Governments and regulatory bodies worldwide have been compelled to revisit existing laws pertaining to surveillance and privacy. Swift amendments were introduced to counterbalance the expansive reach of surveillance programs, bolstering oversight mechanisms and judicial scrutiny to mitigate potential abuses of power. The enduring legacy of Snowden's disclosures is vividly etched in the enactment of legislation aimed at safeguarding individual privacy rights and curtailing unwarranted intrusions into personal data.

From a technological vantage point, the reverberations of Snowden's exposé spurred a wave of innovation focused on harnessing advanced encryption techniques and enhancing digital security measures. Technology firms, in response to mounting concerns over data privacy, intensified their efforts to fortify user data protection protocols and bolster encryption standards, thereby instilling a newfound impetus towards privacy-oriented design and development practices.

In conjunction with these strides, the international arena witnessed a shift in the fabric of data sharing agreements as nations sought to recalibrate their obligations vis-à-vis cross-border data transfers. Snowden's revelations prompted a reevaluation of global data-sharing frameworks, leading to the formulation of revised guidelines and accords that delineate stringent parameters for information exchange while embedding robust safeguards to shield against undue surveillance activities.

However, as we endeavor to gauge the enduring implications of Snowden's disclosures, it is imperative to recognize the complex interplay of interests and factors that continue to mold the contemporary surveillance landscape. While substantial headway has been made in reshaping policies and technologies, the overarching discourse on surveillance, privacy, and state control remains inherently intricate, necessitating ongoing analysis and adaptation to navigate the evolving dynamics of the digital age.

16

Unforeseen Repercussions

Unintended Consequences

The repercussions of Edward Snowden's revelations on the global surveillance apparatus have been both profound and unpredictable. The disclosure of widespread government surveillance programs has triggered a cascade of unintended consequences that have rippled across national security, technology, civil liberties, and international relations. At the core of these unintended outcomes lies the revelation that the pervasive and clandestine nature of surveillance activities has fundamentally shifted the landscape of national security strategy. The initial shockwaves following the disclosures set in motion a series of events that continue to impact our world today. From reevaluating the balance between privacy and security to spurring technological advancements, the snowballing effect of Snowden's actions has underlined the inherent unpredictability of the aftermath of such disclosures. The subsequent reconsideration of intelligence gathering tactics and their implications are themes that permeate numerous aspects of societal change. It becomes evident that even highly classified strategies can be unexpectedly altered when exposed to public scrutiny, creating an intricate web of repercussions that transcend traditional boundaries. Moreover, the dynamic and interconnected nature of the repercussions elucidates how complex systems can yield unanticipated outcomes. National security strategists have been compelled to reassess and recalibrate their approaches in response to the altered threat landscape and the erosion of public trust. This transformative process, influenced by the revelations, has accelerated changes to the methodologies employed by various nations and their intelligence agencies. Exercising caution in tuning policy vehicles is necessary as countries seek to adapt to a new era of digital transparency while safeguarding their interests. As we delve deeper into this chapter, we will discover how the emergent consequences of Snowden's actions have indelibly altered the course of national security strategy, perpetuating implications that resonate far beyond their original context.

Shifts in National Security Strategy

In the wake of Edward Snowden's revelations, national security strategies worldwide underwent significant shifts as governments grappled with the implications of widespread surveillance. The exposed extent of domestic and international surveillance programs sparked a reevaluation of traditional security approaches, triggering a fundamental reconsideration of the balance between privacy and security. This prompted a seismic shift in the intelligence and law enforcement communities, necessitating a reassessment of their methodologies and the legal frameworks governing their activities.

The disclosures led to a realization that the existing framework for collecting and analyzing intelligence required modernization to align with evolving technological capabilities and emerging threats. As such, national security agencies faced the urgent imperative to adapt their operational tactics, harnessing novel technologies and techniques while restructuring their internal procedures to safeguard against future breaches. These changes fundamentally altered the landscape of intelligence gathering and analysis, forcing security entities to re-calibrate their priorities and methods in addressing the increasingly complex global security environment.

Simultaneously, collaboration and information sharing among allied nations witnessed a substantial evolution, with ramifications extending beyond individual countries' borders. The exposure of extensive surveillance partnerships and data-sharing agreements prompted a reconfiguration of international alliances and cooperative efforts in tackling transnational security challenges. Long-standing collaborations were put under scrutiny, and the revelations provoked diplomatic tensions and reshaped global security dynamics, as nations sought to redefine their interconnected roles and responsibilities in safeguarding collective security interests.

Furthermore, the revelations spurred public and political debates regarding the necessity and legitimacy of intrusive surveillance practices in safeguarding national security. Discussions surrounding the intrinsic value of privacy in an age of heightened security concerns permeated political discourse and policy formulation, prompting a reexamination of the societal contract between citizens and the institutions tasked with protecting them. Central to these discussions were ethical considerations and evolving perceptions of civil liberties, influencing legislative measures and shaping the boundaries of permissible state intervention in individuals' private lives.

As national security strategies navigated this profound transformation, they encountered numerous challenges in maintaining a delicate equilibrium between safeguarding citizens and respecting their rights. The repercussions of whistleblower disclosures resounded across diverse arenas, catalyzing an era-defining reorientation in the approach to security, surveillance, and the rights of individuals within contemporary societies.

Economic Implications for Technology Companies

In the wake of Edward Snowden's revelations, technology companies experienced significant economic implications. The exposure of widespread government surveillance raised concerns about the trustworthiness of these companies among both individual consumers and corporate clients. As confidence in the privacy protections offered by technology firms waned, there was a noticeable impact on their bottom lines.

Public perception played a crucial role in shaping this scenario. With the public becoming increasingly aware of potential privacy breaches and unauthorized data access, technology companies faced heightened scrutiny. The erosion of trust resulted in reduced user engagement and a decline in customer acquisition, leading to revenue losses across the industry. Moreover, wary businesses started reevaluating their partnerships and contracts with tech companies, affecting long-term financial projections and contractual obligations.

The aftermath of Snowden's disclosures also compelled technology companies to embark on costly efforts to enhance their security measures and rebuild their tarnished reputations. These endeavors encompassed major investments in encryption technologies, secure communication protocols, and compliance mechanisms to align with evolving data protection regulations. Additionally, companies had to allocate significant resources towards rebuilding trust through transparent communication and proactive disclosure practices concerning their handling of user data.

The economic impact further extended to the global stage, as international markets responded to the revelations. Tech companies faced varying regulatory challenges and market entry barriers amidst growing concerns over surveillance and data privacy, leading to constrained growth opportunities in certain regions. This not only affected the revenue streams of these companies but also reshaped their strategies and resource allocation for expansion.

On a broader scale, the tech industry witnessed a shift in competitive dynamics, with a few players gaining a competitive advantage through their perceived commitment to privacy and security. This increased differentiation in the market fostered a new paradigm where companies were compelled to compete not only on innovation and functionality but also on the strength of their privacy assurances.

Overall, the economic implications for technology companies following the Snowden disclosures were profound and complex, permeating every aspect of their operations – from financial performance and customer relationships to global expansion strategies.

Social Dynamics and Public Trust Reevaluation

In the aftermath of Edward Snowden's revelations, society witnessed a profound reevaluation of public trust in institutions, particularly those involved in intelligence gathering and surveillance. The exposure of extensive data collection programs by government agencies led to widespread skepticism and scrutiny of the state's role in protecting individual privacy and civil liberties. This chapter delves into the intricate social dynamics that arose following the disclosure and the consequential reevaluation of public trust. The unprecedented transparency prompted citizens to question their assumptions about the extent of government oversight and the balance between national security imperatives and individual freedoms. One immediate effect was the erosion of confidence in government agencies, particularly intelligence services, as citizens grappled with the perceived overreach and potential abuse of surveillance capabilities. Moreover, the public began to evaluate the credibility and transparency of tech companies implicated in facilitating mass data collection through their platforms, leading to intensified debates around corporate responsibility and user privacy. Beyond institutional impact, Snowden's revelations precipitated a wave of discourse around the ethical and societal implications of living in an increasingly digitized world. The notion of digital privacy became a focal point as individuals and communities engaged in conversations about the value of personal data, the boundaries of permissible information access, and the responsibilities of both public and private entities in safeguarding sensitive information. These discussions catalyzed a fundamental shift in social norms, redefining expectations and attitudes toward privacy, data security, and government accountability. Furthermore, the disclosures stimulated increased civic engagement and activism, as people worldwide rallied for more transparent and accountable governance, prompting legislative and regulatory reform efforts in many countries. Consequently, the recalibration of public trust sparked a new era of participatory democracy, where citizens sought greater oversight and control in ensuring their rights are preserved within the digital realm.

Intelligence Sharing: New Alliances and Fractures

The disclosure of widespread surveillance activities conducted by intelligence agencies such as the National Security Agency (NSA) through the revelations made by Edward Snowden has dramatically altered the landscape of international intelligence sharing. While traditional alliances among nations were once based on mutual trust and collaboration, the public exposure of extensive data collection programs has strained these relationships and propelled the formation of new alliances. The repercussions of intelligence sharing have been multifaceted, with both positive and negative implications for global security and diplomatic ties.

In the aftermath of the Snowden revelations, trust among allies was significantly undermined, leading to a reevaluation of existing intelligence-sharing arrangements. Longstanding partners in intelligence cooperation expressed deep concern over the extent of the surveillance practices revealed, raising questions about the boundaries of acceptable conduct in gathering intelligence. This scrutiny resulted in strains on erstwhile alliances, sparking a reconfiguration of the geopolitical landscape as countries sought to reassess their strategic partnerships and reestablish trust.

Conversely, the disclosures also paved the way for the forging of new alliances driven by a shared commitment to protect privacy and civil liberties. Nations disillusioned by the overreach of certain intelligence-sharing accords sought to align themselves with like-minded counterparts, fostering a fresh wave of collaboration centered around safeguarding individual freedoms from unwarranted intrusion. This realignment of international relationships brought about a renaissance in intelligence diplomacy, typified by concerted efforts to promote transparency, accountability, and respect for human rights within the realm of surveillance and data collection.

Amid these significant shifts in alliance structures, fractures emerged within previously cohesive coalitions, stemming from differing perspectives on the appropriate balance between security imperatives and privacy rights. Disagreements over the use of mass surveillance technologies and the scope of information gathering capabilities incited internal divisions among allies, as some nations advocated for stringent reforms while others defended the status quo. These schisms have engendered complex dynamics within the intelligence community, giving rise to new fault lines that have the potential to reshape the geopolitical order.

As intelligence-sharing mechanisms continue to evolve in the wake of the Snowden disclosures, the international landscape is marked by a delicate interplay of rejuvenated partnerships, strained alliances, and embryonic ententes. The repercussions of these developments resonate across diplomatic circles, shaping the contours of intelligence cooperation and wielding profound influence over the future of global security and privacy governance.

Impacts on Civil Liberties and Privacy Law

The disclosures made by Edward Snowden regarding mass surveillance programs have triggered profound impacts on civil liberties and privacy laws. These revelations led to heightened scrutiny of government surveillance practices, raising fundamental questions about the balance between national security interests and individual rights. One of the most significant impacts is the reevaluation and reformulation of existing legislation and policies aimed at safeguarding civil liberties and privacy. In response to public outcry and mounting concerns over privacy infringement, various legislative measures have been proposed and enacted to enhance oversight of intelligence agencies and limit their surveillance capabilities. As a result, unprecedented debates and legal battles have unfolded, igniting discussions on constitutional rights and governmental transparency. Furthermore, judicial review and landmark court rulings have reshaped the legal landscape, setting crucial precedents in defining the boundaries of surveillance activities by the state. The implications of these developments extend beyond domestic jurisdiction, influencing global conversations on privacy protection and international human rights standards. Privacy laws and regulations have undergone substantial revisions, reflecting an evolving understanding of privacy in the digital age and aiming to address the complexities posed by advancing technology. Additionally, the impact on civil liberties and privacy law is intricately linked to broader societal shifts in perceptions of personal privacy, data protection, and individual autonomy. The widespread dissemination of Snowden's revelations has galvanized public awareness and activism, prompting individuals and organizations to demand greater accountability and transparency from governments and corporations. This collective consciousness has propelled the emergence of advocacy initiatives and grassroots movements advocating for privacy rights and civil liberties protections. Simultaneously, it has catalyzed innovative approaches to encryption, cybersecurity, and digital self-defense, empowering individuals to safeguard their privacy in an era of pervasive surveillance. Overall, the reverberations of Edward Snowden's disclosures continue to resonate profoundly, as they provoke ongoing discourse and decisive actions to redefine the interplay between civil liberties, privacy law, and governmental authority in the 21st century.

Cybersecurity Measures: Enhancement or Overreach?

The debate surrounding cybersecurity measures in the aftermath of surveillance disclosures has been intense and multifaceted. On one hand, governments and intelligence agencies argue that enhanced cybersecurity measures are essential to safeguard national security interests, protect critical infrastructure, and combat cyber threats from hostile actors. This perspective advocates for increased surveillance capabilities, data collection, and monitoring as crucial tools in the fight against cybercrime, terrorism, and espionage. Proponents of this view emphasize the necessity of staying ahead of rapidly evolving technological advancements and the growing sophistication of malicious cyber activities.

Conversely, critics of expansive cybersecurity measures raise concerns about potential overreach and encroachment on individual privacy rights and civil liberties. They contend that unchecked surveillance and data-gathering initiatives may lead to unwarranted intrusion into the lives of law-abiding citizens, creating a chilling effect on free expression, association, and dissent. Furthermore, the indiscriminate collection and retention of vast amounts of personal information could pose substantial risks if abused or compromised, possibly resulting in widespread privacy violations and vulnerabilities. This counterargument underscores the importance of striking a balance between security imperatives and the protection of fundamental rights.

Amidst these opposing perspectives, the implications of cybersecurity measures extend beyond national borders, influencing global norms and relationships. Questions arise regarding the potential impact on diplomatic relations, international cooperation, and the trust between nations. The dynamics of cybersecurity governance, information sharing, and collaborative efforts to address cyber threats in a transparent and accountable manner become critical considerations in shaping the future landscape of digital security.

Moreover, the convergence of cybersecurity and human rights concerns necessitates careful evaluation of the ethical and legal dimensions underpinning digital defense strategies. As technological innovations continue to reshape the digital realm, it is imperative to engage in constructive dialogue and policymaking processes that are responsive to evolving challenges while upholding democratic values and the rule of law. Ultimately, the ongoing discourse on cybersecurity measures reflects the complex intersections of security, liberty, and accountability in an interconnected and digitized world.

Media's Evolving Role in Surveillance Disclosure

The media has played a pivotal role in shaping public discourse and understanding regarding Edward Snowden's unprecedented disclosures of government surveillance programs. Not only did the revelations trigger widespread debates on matters of privacy, civil liberties, and national security, but they also ignited intense discussions about the responsibilities and ethics of journalism in the digital age. As media organizations grappled with the magnitude and sensitivity of the leaked information, they faced profound ethical dilemmas and operational challenges. The nature of reporting on classified material posed complex questions about the public's right to know versus potential harm to national security. It forced reevaluations of traditional journalistic norms and practices, ultimately leading to a transformation in the reporting landscape. Journalists and media outlets had to navigate the delicate balance between informing the public and safeguarding sensitive information, all while under the scrutiny of government pressures and public opinion. Some outlets collaborated with intelligence agencies to carefully redact sensitive details before publication, while others took a more confrontational approach, choosing to publish the information in its entirety. This diversity of strategies underscored the decentralized and autonomous nature of journalistic decision-making and editorial responsibility. Simultaneously, the rise of digital media and social networks redefined the dissemination of news, enabling whistleblowers, citizen journalists, and independent media platforms to bypass traditional gatekeepers and contribute to the public discourse. The immediacy and reach of these new channels brought both liberation and complication, presenting uncharted opportunities for fostering transparency and accountability, yet also facilitating the spread of misinformation and propaganda. Moreover, as the boundaries between journalism and advocacy blurred, discussions arose about the role of journalism in fostering civic participation and protecting democratic values. The impact of Snowden's disclosures not only transformed the content and methods of investigative reporting but also provoked critical questions about the relationship between media, government, and the public. The evolving role of the media in surveillance disclosure has undoubtedly reshaped the dynamics of accountability, transparency, and the pursuit of truth, laying the groundwork for a redefined era of investigative journalism and information dissemination.

Emergence of Encryption and Anonymity Tools

The revelations brought to light by the Snowden disclosures ignited a seismic shift in the digital landscape, particularly in the realms of privacy and security. This paradigm upheaval spurred an unprecedented proliferation of encryption and anonymity tools designed to empower individuals and organizations to protect their sensitive data from unwarranted intrusion. In response to pervasive surveillance practices, enterprising technologists and privacy advocates spearheaded the development of robust encryption methods that could shield communications from prying eyes. This surge in innovative solutions amplified the availability and accessibility of encryption technologies, facilitating widespread adoption across diverse user segments. Amid growing concerns over government overreach and corporate data mining, these tools became indispensable for preserving digital confidentiality and fortifying information integrity. Arguably, this marked the dawn of a new era where privacy-conscious individuals sought refuge behind cryptographic shields to reclaim sovereignty over their digital footprints. Furthermore, the emergence of anonymity tools - such as virtual private networks (VPNs) and anonymous browsing platforms - furnished users with the means to obfuscate their online activities and obscure their digital identities. These tools leveraged sophisticated tactics to conceal users' IP addresses, thwart surveillance measures, and navigate cyberspace incognito. Catalyzed by Snowden's disclosures, uptake of these anonymizing technologies surged, epitomizing a societal drive towards safeguarding online interactions from unwarranted eavesdropping and monitoring. The confluence of these technological innovations impelled a profound reconfiguration of internet usage, as individuals and entities increasingly prioritized safeguarding their digital communications and interactions. While heralding a pivotal evolution in the digital realm, the ascent of encryption and anonymity tools underscored the intensifying urgency to fortify data protection protocols and bolster cybersecurity defenses. Nevertheless, this burgeoning trend also galvanized contentious debates surrounding lawful access to encrypted communications, prompting deliberations on the inherent tensions between security imperatives and individual privacy rights. As the specter of mass surveillance persisted, the ascent of these protective measures radiated ripples throughout the digital ecosystem, redefining perceptions of online privacy and recalibrating the power dynamics governing information dissemination.

Conclusion: Summarizing Unintended Outcomes

The emergence of encryption and anonymity tools in the aftermath of Edward Snowden's revelations has marked a significant shift in the landscape of digital privacy and security. As we conclude our exploration of the unintended repercussions stemming from Snowden's disclosure, it is essential to reflect on the broader implications of this profound transformation.

One of the most remarkable unintended outcomes has been the rapid proliferation and diversification of encryption technologies. This widespread adoption represents a direct response to the public's heightened awareness regarding online surveillance and data privacy. Companies, governments, and individuals are increasingly turning to encryption to safeguard their communications and sensitive information from unauthorized access.

Anonymity tools, including virtual private networks (VPNs) and secure messaging platforms, have also experienced a surge in popularity. These tools empower users to obfuscate their digital footprint and protect their identities from surveillance and tracking. While these developments have undoubtedly bolstered the individual's ability to maintain privacy in the digital realm, they have also posed challenges for law enforcement and intelligence agencies in their efforts to gather crucial intelligence and prevent illicit activities.

Furthermore, the widespread adoption of encryption and anonymity tools has led to a paradigm shift in cybersecurity practices. Organizations and governments around the world are revising their approaches to digital defense, as traditional methods of interception and analysis become less effective in the face of encrypted communications. This shift has prompted a reevaluation of national security strategies, with an increasing emphasis on proactive threat prevention and innovative approaches to intelligence gathering.

However, the widespread use of encryption and anonymity tools has also raised concerns about their potential misuse by malicious actors. In response, legislative bodies and policymakers have grappled with the challenge of striking a balance between privacy protection and national security imperatives. The debate surrounding encryption backdoors and lawful access mechanisms remains contentious, reflecting the complex ethical and practical considerations at play.

Moreover, the emergence of encryption and anonymity tools has fundamentally transformed the dynamics of global intelligence sharing. Traditional alliances have been strained, and new collaborative efforts have emerged to address mutual challenges in the digital domain. As nations navigate this evolving landscape, questions of trust, reciprocity, and sovereignty have assumed new significance in shaping international relations and cooperation.

In conclusion, the unintended repercussions of Edward Snowden's disclosures have reshaped the digital landscape in profound ways. The widespread adoption of encryption and anonymity tools has catalyzed a paradigm shift in digital privacy, cybersecurity, and global intelligence dynamics. As we navigate the complexities of this transformed terrain, it is imperative to engage in informed dialogue and ethical deliberation to reconcile competing interests and chart a path forward that upholds both security and fundamental rights.

17

Revelations Uncovered: Snowden's Exposé

In the aftermath of Edward Snowden's unprecedented disclosures, the global landscape of surveillance underwent a dramatic and far-reaching transformation that continues to reverberate through the realms of governance, technology, and human rights. The seismic shift in public awareness precipitated by Snowden's revelations thrust the intricate interplay between security imperatives and individual liberties into sharp relief, catalyzing a profound reevaluation of the ethical, legal, and societal dimensions of surveillance.

The revelations of mass data collection and pervasive surveillance practices by intelligence agencies engendered a watershed moment in the annals of modern history, unearthing the pernicious implications of unchecked executive power and the erosion of fundamental rights. The unprecedented depth and breadth of surveillance practices unveiled by Snowden served as a wake-up call, shattering the veneer of complacency and catalyzing a resolute demand for the recalibration of the surveillance landscape to harmonize with democratic principles and human rights imperatives.

The intricate dance between security imperatives and privacy rights pervades the fabric of democratic governance, enkindling a steadfast resolve to fortify the delicate balance between these seemingly conflicting prerogatives. The swift and resolute response elicited by Snowden's disclosures galvanized a groundswell of demands for robust legal and regulatory safeguards, compelling governments to enact comprehensive oversight mechanisms and stringent judicial review processes to rein in the specter of unchecked surveillance. The imperative of transparency and accountability burgeoned as a guiding beacon, illuminating the path toward a rights-centered surveillance framework that strikes an equilibrium between national security exigencies and individual freedoms.

The advancement of digital technologies and the proliferation of digital communications fostered a daunting quandary regarding the contours of permissible surveillance within the digital domain, precipitating an exigent need to delineate the boundaries of surveillance practices in alignment with ethical and legal precepts. The ascendancy of encryption and privacy-enhancing technologies crystallized as a linchpin in fortifying the digital defenses of individuals and organizations, conferring a potent armor against unauthorized access and data exploitation. The harmonization of technological innovations and privacy safeguards coalesced as a pivotal imperative, delineating the imperative of harnessing innovation in the service of individual empowerment and the protection of fundamental rights.

The confluence of technological advancements and ethical imperatives underscored the inextricable linkage between innovation and the protection of individual liberties in the digital age, fueling a clarion call for a renaissance of ethical surveillance practices. Deliberations within international fora and legislative chambers grappled with the complex interplay between security exigencies and individual rights, confronting the myriad ethical conundrums intertwined with the surveillance apparatus. The conception of a rights-respecting surveillance regime emerged as a guiding lodestar, steering the recalibration of national security frameworks to harmonize with the imperatives of democracy, accountability, and human rights.

Edward Snowden's audacious act served as a catalyst for a wholesale reevaluation of the underlying ethical underpinnings of government surveillance, spurring a candid reckoning of the profound moral implications of pervasive surveillance. The enduring legacy of Snowden's seismic disclosures reverberates as a cautionary tale, compelling a sustained and conscientious commitment to upholding the sanctity of individual rights in the face of emergent security challenges. Snowden's indelible impact stands as a testament to the catalytic power of individual agency in reshaping the contours of governance and fortifying the foundational principles of democratic society.

As the global community navigates the complex terrain of surveillance reform, the imperatives of fostering multi-stakeholder dialogues and international cooperation burgeon as linchpins in crafting a harmonized approach to reconciling security imperatives with individual liberties. The ascendancy of interoperable legal frameworks and transnational partnerships crystallize as pivotal levers in harmonizing the complex mosaic of surveillance practices across borders, fortifying the tapestry of global governance. The resounding ethos of transparency and accountability burgeons as a lodestar in shaping the contours of surveillance, carving a path toward a rights-respecting and globally harmonized surveillance regime.

The ascendancy of emerging technologies and the inexorable march of digital transformation engender an imperative for conscientious stewardship of ethical principles in the realm of surveillance. The emergent frontiers of surveillance, forged in the crucible of technological innovation, amplify the ethical imperatives underlying the responsible deployment of surveillance capabilities. The ascendancy of ethical frameworks and the infusion of human rights considerations offer a guidepost in navigating the ethical labyrinth of surveillance, steering the trajectory of surveillance practices toward a rights-respecting and morally conscientious paradigm.

As the pendulum of surveillance reform swings toward a rights-centered arc, the imperative of cultivating a culture of digital literacy and privacy awareness burgeons as a cornerstone in fortifying the resilience of individuals and communities against unwarranted intrusions.

The ascendancy of privacy education and the promulgation of digital literacy programs crystallize as pivotal tools in equipping individuals with the knowledge to safeguard their digital footprints and navigate the complex terrain of digital surveillance. The cultivation of a robust ecosystem of privacy-conscious individuals and organizations constitutes a linchpin in erecting a bulwark against the encroachment of unwarranted surveillance practices, fostering a landscape of empowered digital citizenship.

The enduring legacy of Edward Snowden's seismic revelations compels a sustained reevaluation of the ethical, legal, and societal dimensions of surveillance, galvanizing a resolute commitment to fortify the edifice of human rights and civil liberties in the digital age. Snowden's indelible impact echoes as a clarion call for unwavering vigilance in preserving the delicate equilibrium between security imperatives and individual freedoms, underscoring the contemplative imperative of charting a principled path toward a rights-respecting and democratic surveillance regime.

18

Continuing Controversy: The Enduring Debate

Edward Snowden's decision to blow the whistle on the extensive surveillance practices of the United States government was a pivotal and highly controversial moment in the ongoing discourse on privacy, security, and the boundaries of governmental authority. Snowden's revelations provided a rare and unprecedented glimpse into the inner workings of mass surveillance programs, raising profound questions about the balance between national security imperatives and the protection of individual liberties.

The extensive cache of classified documents that Snowden made public shed light on the vast scope and reach of surveillance activities conducted by government agencies both domestically and internationally. Programs such as PRISM and XKeyscore, revealed through the leaked documents, underscored the scale of data collection and monitoring, sparking widespread concern and condemnation.

In the wake of Snowden's exposé, governments, civil society, and technology companies were compelled to reevaluate their roles and responsibilities in shaping the ethical and legal contours of surveillance.

The revelations prompted a closer examination of the legal frameworks underpinning surveillance activities, spurring international debates on the need for robust oversight, transparency, and accountability in intelligence and law enforcement operations.

At its core, Snowden's whistleblowing initiative served as a catalyst for critical global conversations around the protection of privacy and civil liberties in the digital age. The disclosure of the widespread collection and analysis of digital communications data underscored the profound implications of unchecked surveillance on the rights and freedoms of individuals, prompting a reevaluation of the societal tacit acceptance of mass data collection practices.

The fallout from Snowden's revelations extended to the domain of technology and corporate responsibility, with major tech companies facing heightened scrutiny over their roles in facilitating government access to user data. These revelations triggered a wave of introspection within the technology sector, leading to an increased emphasis on implementing robust encryption measures, advocating for user privacy rights, and enhancing transparency in handling government requests for data.

Furthermore, Snowden's exposé prompted a wave of legislative and judicial actions aimed at reining in unchecked surveillance activities and fortifying the legal protections of individual privacy rights. Landmark court cases and legislative reforms in multiple countries served as a direct response to the revelations, highlighting the imperative to establish clear boundaries and safeguards for governmental surveillance powers.

Notably, the reverberations of Snowden's actions continue to manifest in the ongoing efforts to strike a delicate balance between national security imperatives and the rights of individuals to privacy and due process. The enduring legacy of Snowden's whistleblowing serves as a poignant reminder of the enduring need to confront the moral and ethical dimensions of modern surveillance practices in an interconnected world, as well as to uphold the fundamental rights and dignity of all individuals in the digital age. This ongoing discussion has led to the development of privacy-enhancing technologies, stronger regulations, and international agreements focused on protecting individual privacy rights in an increasingly interconnected and digital world. This shift has not only had an impact on government surveillance practices but has also influenced the way companies handle user data and the expectations of individuals regarding their digital privacy. The Snowden revelations have also prompted a reevaluation of the relationship between technology and democracy, encouraging a reassessment of the power dynamics between citizens, governments, and the private sector in the context of digital rights and freedoms.

The public discourse ignited by Snowden's actions prompted a broader examination of the implications of government surveillance and raised awareness about the need for transparency and accountability in national security policies. It also brought attention to the global nature of surveillance, with implications for individuals and organizations worldwide. As a result, international collaboration and cooperation on privacy and surveillance issues have gained prominence, leading to initiatives aimed at defining global standards for the responsible and ethical use of surveillance technologies and data collection practices.

In addition, Snowden's disclosures have had a lasting impact on the public's perception of privacy and surveillance. They have served as a wake-up call, prompting individuals to become more aware of the digital footprint they leave behind and the potential vulnerabilities associated with widespread data collection. This heightened awareness has fostered a growing demand for tools and services that prioritize privacy and security, leading to a burgeoning market for privacy-focused products and initiatives aimed at empowering individuals to protect their personal information in the digital realm.

Moreover, the Snowden revelations have sparked a reevaluation of the role of whistleblowers in modern society and the moral complexities inherent in exposing classified information. Snowden's own journey as a whistleblower has become a pivotal case study in discussions surrounding dissent, government transparency, and individual conscience, prompting introspection on the ethical obligations of individuals working within institutions of power.

The enduring legacy of Edward Snowden's courageous act continues to resonate, shaping the ongoing discourse on privacy, surveillance, and individual freedoms in the digital age. It has sparked a global awakening to the complexities and implications of unchecked surveillance, igniting conversations that transcend national borders and envision a world in which the rights and dignity of individuals are safeguarded in the face of evolving technological and security challenges.

www.ingramcontent.com/pod-product-compliance
Lightning Source LLC
Chambersburg PA
CBHW051723020426
42333CB00014B/1119